I0276005

MznLnx

Missing Links Exam Preps

Exam Prep for

Management A Practical Introduction

Kinicki, Williams, 2nd Edition

The MznLnx Exam Prep is your link from the texbook and lecture to your exams.
The MznLnx Exam Preps are unauthorized and comprehensive reviews of your textbooks.

All material provided by MznLnx and Rico Publications (c) 2010
Textbook publishers and textbook authors do not particpate in or contribute to these reviews.

MznLnx

Rico
Publications

Exam Prep for Management A Practical Introduction
2nd Edition
Kinicki, Williams

Publisher: Raymond Houge
Assistant Editor: Michael Rouger
Text and Cover Designer: Lisa Buckner
Marketing Manager: Sara Swagger
Project Manager, Editorial Production: Jerry Emerson
Art Director: Vernon Lowerui
Product Manager: Dave Mason
Editorial Assitant: Rachel Guzmanji
Pedagogy: Debra Long
Cover Image: Jim Reed/Getty Images
Text and Cover Printer: City Printing, Inc.
Compositor: Media Mix, Inc.

(c) 2010 Rico Publications
ALL RIGHTS RESERVED. No part of this work covered by the copyright may be reproduced or used in any form or by an means--graphic, electronic, or mechanical, including photocopying, recording, taping, Web distribution, information storage, and retrieval systems, or in any other manner--without the written permission of the publisher.

For more information about our products, contact us at:
Dave.Mason@RicoPublications.com

For permission to use material from this text or product, submit a request online to:
Dave.Mason@RicoPublications.com

Printed in the United States
ISBN:

Contents

TO THE STUDENT

COMPREHENSIVE

The *MznLnx* Exam Prep series is designed to help you pass your exams. Editors at MznLnx review your textbooks and then prepare these practice exams to help you master the textbook material. Unlike study guides, workbooks, and practice tests provided by the texbook publisher and textbook authors, *MznLnx* gives you ***all*** of the material in each chapter in exam form, not just samples, so you can be sure to nail your exam.

MECHANICAL

The MznLnx Exam Prep series creates exams that will help you learn the subject matter as well as test you on your understanding. Each question is designed to help you master the concept. Just working through the exams, you gain an understanding of the subject--its a simple mechanical process that produces success.

INTEGRATED STUDY GUIDE AND REVIEW

MznLnx is not just a set of exams designed to test you, its also a comprehensive review of the subject content. Each exam question is also a review of the concept, making sure that you will get the answer correct without having to go to other sources of material. You learn as you go! Its the easiest way to pass an exam.

HUMOR

Studying can be tedious and dry. MznLnx's instructional design includes moderate humor within the exam questions on occassion, to break the tedium and revitalize the brain

1. _________ is a term defined by the Oxford English Dictionary as an individual's 'course or progress through life '. It is usually considered to pertain to remunerative work (and sometimes also formal education.)

The etymology of the term is somewhat ironic in that it comes from the Latin word carrera, which means race .

a. Nursing shortage
b. Spatial mismatch
c. Career planning
d. Career

2. _________ has been described as the 'process of social influence in which one person can enlist the aid and support of others in the accomplishment of a common task' . A definition more inclusive of followers comes from Alan Keith of Genentech who said '_________ is ultimately about creating a way for people to contribute to making something extraordinary happen.'

_________ is one of the most salient aspects of the organizational context. However, defining _________ has been challenging.

a. 1990 Clean Air Act
b. Leadership
c. Situational leadership
d. 28-hour day

3. The _________ (Situation, Task, Action, Result) format is a job interview technique used by interviewers to gather all the relevant information about a specific capability that the job requires. This interview format is said to have a higher degree of predictability of future on-the-job performance than the traditional interview.

- Situation: The interviewer wants you to present a recent challenge and situation in which you found yourself.
- Task: What did you have to achieve? The interviewer will be looking to see what you were trying to achieve from the situation.
- Action: What did you do? The interviewer will be looking for information on what you did, why you did it and what were the alternatives.
- Results: What was the outcome of your actions? What did you achieve through your actions and did you meet your objectives. What did you learn from this experience and have you used this learning since?

.

a. Rasch models
b. Phrase completion
c. Competency-based job descriptions
d. Star

4. _________ is the process of learning a new skill or trade, often in response to a change in the economic environment. Generally it reflects changes in profession choice rather than an 'upward' movement in the same field.

There is some controversy surrounding the use of _________ to offset economic changes caused by free trade and automation.

a. Suspension training
b. Krauthammer
c. Compliance Training
d. Retraining

5. _________ is a mathematical science pertaining to the collection, analysis, interpretation or explanation, and presentation of data. It also provides tools for prediction and forecasting based on data. It is applicable to a wide variety of academic disciplines, from the natural and social sciences to the humanities, government and business.

a. Failure rate
b. Location parameter
c. Simple moving average
d. Statistics

6. A _________ is a compensation, usually financial, received by a worker in exchange for their labor.

Compensation in terms of _________s is given to worker and compensation in terms of salary is given to employees. Compensation is a monetary benefits given to employees in returns of the services provided by them.

a. Wage
b. Performance-related pay
c. Profit-sharing agreement
d. State Compensation Insurance Fund

7. _________ is, in very basic words, a position a firm occupies against its competitors.

According to Michael Porter, the three methods for creating a sustainable _________ are through:

1. Cost leadership

2. Differentiation

3. Focus (economics)

a. 1990 Clean Air Act
b. 28-hour day
c. Theory Z
d. Competitive advantage

8. The 'business case for _________', theorizes that in a global marketplace, a company that employs a diverse workforce (both men and women, people of many generations, people from ethnically and racially diverse backgrounds etc.) is better able to understand the demographics of the marketplace it serves and is thus better equipped to thrive in that marketplace than a company that has a more limited range of employee demographics.

An additional corollary suggests that a company that supports the _________ of its workforce can also improve employee satisfaction, productivity and retention.

a. Kanban
b. Virtual team
c. Diversity
d. Trademark

9. _________ is the point where a person stops employment completely. A person may also semi-retire and keep some sort of _________ job, out of choice rather than necessity. This usually happens upon reaching a determined age, when physical conditions don't allow the person to work any more (by illness or accident), or even for personal choice (usually in the presence of an adequate pension or personal savings.)

a. Severance package
b. Termination of employment
c. Wrongful dismissal
d. Retirement

10. _________ is a business magazine published by McGraw-Hill. It was first published in 1929 (as The Business Week) under the direction of Malcolm Muir, who was serving as president of the McGraw-Hill Publishing company at the time. Its primary competitors in the national business magazine category are Fortune and Forbes, which are published bi-weekly.

a. Hotel Vikas
b. The Wealth of Nations
c. BusinessWeek
d. Democracy in America

11. _________, commonly referred to as 'eBusiness' or 'e-Business', may be defined as the utilization of information and communication technologies (ICT) in support of all the activities of business. Commerce constitutes the exchange of products and services between businesses, groups and individuals and hence can be seen as one of the essential activities of any business. Hence, electronic commerce or eCommerce focuses on the use of ICT to enable the external activities and relationships of the business with individuals, groups and other businesses .

a. A4e
b. A Stake in the Outcome
c. AAAI
d. Electronic business

12. _________, commonly known as e-commerce, consists of the buying and selling of products or services over electronic systems such as the Internet and other computer networks. The amount of trade conducted electronically has grown extraordinarily with widespread Internet usage. The use of commerce is conducted in this way, spurring and drawing on innovations in electronic funds transfer, supply chain management, Internet marketing, online transaction processing, electronic data interchange (EDI), inventory management systems, and automated data collection systems.

a. A4e
b. Electronic Commerce
c. A Stake in the Outcome
d. Online shopping

13. _________ in its literal sense is the process of transformation of local or regional phenomena into global ones. It can be described as a process by which the people of the world are unified into a single society and function together.

This process is a combination of economic, technological, sociocultural and political forces.

a. Collaborative Planning, Forecasting and Replenishment
b. Histogram
c. Cost Management
d. Globalization

14. _________ refers to the movement of cash into or out of a business or financial product. It is usually measured during a specified, finite period of time. Measurement of _________ can be used

- to determine a project's rate of return or value. The time of _________s into and out of projects are used as inputs in financial models such as internal rate of return, and net present value.
- to determine problems with a business's liquidity. Being profitable does not necessarily mean being liquid. A company can fail because of a shortage of cash, even while profitable.
- as an alternate measure of a business's profits when it is believed that accrual accounting concepts do not represent economic realities. For example, a company may be notionally profitable but generating little operational cash (as may be the case for a company that barters its products rather than selling for cash.) In such a case, the company may be deriving additional operating cash by issuing shares evaluating default risk, re-investment requirements, etc.

_________ is a generic term used differently depending on the context. It may be defined by users for their own purposes.

a. Gross profit
b. Sweat equity
c. Cash flow
d. Gross profit margin

15. _________ is the discipline of planning, organizing and managing resources to bring about the successful completion of specific project goals and objectives. It is often closely related to and sometimes conflated with Program management.

A project is a finite endeavor--having specific start and completion dates--undertaken to meet particular goals and objectives, usually to bring about beneficial change or added value.

a. Project management
b. Work package
c. Project engineer
d. Precedence diagram

16. A _________ -- also known as a geographically dispersed team -- is a group of individuals who work across time, space, and organizational boundaries with links strengthened by webs of communication technology. They have complementary skills and are committed to a common purpose, have interdependent performance goals, and share an approach to work for which they hold themselves mutually accountable. Geographically dispersed teams allow organizations to hire and retain the best people regardless of location.

a. Kanban
b. Trademark
c. Risk management
d. Virtual team

17. _________ comprises a range of practices used in an organisation to identify, create, represent, distribute and enable adoption of insights and experiences. Such insights and experiences comprise knowledge, either embodied in individuals or embedded in organisational processes or practice.

An established discipline since 1991 , _________ includes courses taught in the fields of business administration, information systems, management, and library and information sciences .

a. 1990 Clean Air Act
b. 28-hour day
c. 33 Strategies of War
d. Knowledge management

18. A _________ is the term given to a company that facilitates the learning of its members and continuously transforms itself. _________s develop as a result of the pressures facing modern organizations and enables them to remain competitive in the business environment. A _________ has five main features; systems thinking, personal mastery, mental models, shared vision and team learning.

a. Learning organization
b. Hoshin Kanri
c. Quality function deployment
d. 1990 Clean Air Act

19. _________, e-commuting, e-work, telework, working from home (WFH), or working at home (WAH) is a work arrangement in which employees enjoy flexibility in working location and hours. In other words, the daily commute to a central place of work is replaced by telecommunication links. Many work from home, while others, occasionally also referred to as nomad workers or web commuters utilize mobile telecommunications technology to work from coffee shops or myriad other locations.

a. 33 Strategies of War
b. 28-hour day
c. 1990 Clean Air Act
d. Telecommuting

20. _________ is a process of planning and controlling the performance or execution of any type of activity, such as:

- a project (project _________) or
- a process (process _________, sometimes referred to as the process performance measurement and management system.)

Organization's senior management is responsible for carrying out its _________.

a. Participatory management
b. Work design
c. Management process
d. Human Relations Movement

21. A _________ or maquila is a factory that imports materials and equipment on a duty-free and tariff-free basis for assembly or manufacturing and then re-exports the assembled product, usually back to the originating country. A maquila is also referred to as a 'twin plant', or 'in-bond' industry. Nearly half a million Mexicans are employed in _________s.

a. 33 Strategies of War
b. 28-hour day
c. 1990 Clean Air Act
d. Maquiladora

22. A _________ is a type of business entity in which partners (owners) share with each other the profits or losses of the business. _________s are often favored over corporations for taxation purposes, as the _________ structure does not generally incur a tax on profits before it is distributed to the partners (i.e. there is no dividend tax levied.) However, depending on the _________ structure and the jurisdiction in which it operates, owners of a _________ may be exposed to greater personal liability than they would as shareholders of a corporation.

a. Due process
b. Federal Employers Liability Act
c. Partnership
d. Mediation

23. A _________ is a list of the general tasks and responsibilities of a position. Typically, it also includes to whom the position reports, specifications such as the qualifications needed by the person in the job, salary range for the position, etc. A _________ is usually developed by conducting a job analysis, which includes examining the tasks and sequences of tasks necessary to perform the job.

a. Recruitment Process Insourcing
b. Recruitment advertising
c. Recruitment
d. Job description

24. _________ is an idea in the field of Organizational studies and management which describes the psychology, attitudes, experiences, beliefs and Values (personal and cultural values) of an organization. It has been defined as 'the specific collection of values and norms that are shared by people and groups in an organization and that control the way they interact with each other and with stakeholders outside the organization.'

This definition continues to explain organizational values also known as 'beliefs and ideas about what kinds of goals members of an organization should pursue and ideas about the appropriate kinds or standards of behavior organizational members should use to achieve these goals. From organizational values develop organizational norms, guidelines or expectations that prescribe appropriate kinds of behavior by employees in particular situations and control the behavior of organizational members towards one another.'

_________ is not the same as corporate culture.

a. Organizational effectiveness
b. Union shop
c. Organizational culture
d. Organizational development

25. A _________ or chief executive is one of the highest-ranking corporate officer (executive) or administrator in charge of total management. An individual selected as President and _________ of a corporation, company, organization, or agency, reports to the board of directors. In internal communication and press releases, many companies capitalize the term and those of other high positions, even when they are not proper nouns.

a. Chief executive officer
b. Financial analyst
c. Purchasing manager
d. Chief brand officer

26. A _________ or chief operations officer is a corporate officer responsible for managing the day-to-day activities of the corporation and for operations management (OM.) The _________ is one of the highest-ranking members of an organization's senior management, monitoring the daily operations of the company and reporting to the board of directors and the top executive officer, usually the chief executive officer (CEO.) The _________ is usually an executive or senior officer.

a. Chief operating officer
b. Supervisory board
c. Product innovation
d. Value based pricing

27. A _________ in today's workforce is an individual that is valued for their ability to interpret information within a specific subject area. They will often advance the overall understanding of that subject through focused analysis, design and/or development. They use research skills to define problems and to identify alternatives.

a. Business rule
b. Career development
c. Customer satisfaction
d. Knowledge worker

28. _________ are, simply put, various approaches or ways of learning. They involve educating methods, particular to an individual, that are presumed to allow that individual to learn best. It is commonly believed that most people favor some particular method of interacting with, taking in, and processing stimuli or information.

a. 1990 Clean Air Act
b. 33 Strategies of War
c. 28-hour day
d. Learning styles

29. While _________ literally refers to a person responsible for the performance of duties involved in running an organization, the exact meaning of the role is variable, depending on the organization.

While there is no clear line between executive or principal and inferior officers, principal officers are high-level officials in the executive branch of U.S. government such as department heads of independent agencies. In Humphrey's Executor v. United States, 295 U.S. 602 (1935), the Court distinguished between _________s and quasi-legislative or quasi-judicial officers by stating that the former serve at the pleasure of the President and may be removed at his discretion.

a. Easement
b. Executive officer
c. Australian Fair Pay and Conditions Standard
d. Unreported employment

30. _________ for short is a descriptive term for certain executives in a business operation. It is also a formal title held by some business executives, most commonly in the hospitality industry.

A _________ has broad, overall responsibility for a business or organization. Whereas a manager may be responsible for one functional area, the _________ is responsible for all areas.

a. Chief knowledge officer
b. Chief technology officer
c. Managing director
d. General manager

31. _________ is a method by which the job performance of an employee is evaluated _________ is a part of career development.

_________s are regular reviews of employee performance within organizations

Generally, the aims of a _________ are to:

- Give feedback on performance to employees.
- Identify employee training needs.
- Document criteria used to allocate organizational rewards.
- Form a basis for personnel decisions: salary increases, promotions, disciplinary actions, etc.
- Provide the opportunity for organizational diagnosis and development.
- Facilitate communication between employee and administraton
- Validate selection techniques and human resource policies to meet federal Equal Employment Opportunity requirements.

A common approach to assessing performance is to use a numerical or scalar rating system whereby managers are asked to score an individual against a number of objectives/attributes. In some companies, employees receive assessments from their manager, peers, subordinates and customers while also performing a self assessment.

a. Human resource management
b. Progressive discipline
c. Personnel management
d. Performance appraisal

32. _________ can be regarded as an outcome of mental processes (cognitive process) leading to the selection of a course of action among several alternatives. Every _________ process produces a final choice. The output can be an action or an opinion of choice.

a. Decision making
b. 1990 Clean Air Act
c. 28-hour day
d. 33 Strategies of War

33. _________ refers to the process of screening, and selecting qualified people for a job at an organization or firm mid- and large-size organizations and companies often retain professional recruiters or outsource some of the process to _________ agencies. External _________ is the process of attracting and selecting employees from outside the organization.

The _________ industry has four main types of agencies: employment agencies, _________ websites and job search engines, 'headhunters' for executive and professional _________, and in-house _________.

a. Labour hire
b. Referral recruitment
c. Recruitment
d. Recruitment Process Outsourcing

34. An _________ is a person who has possession of an enterprise and assumes significant accountability for the inherent risks and the outcome. It is an ambitious leader who combines land, labor, and capital to create and market new goods or services. The term is a loanword from French and was first defined by the Irish economist Richard Cantillon.

a. A4e
b. AAAI
c. A Stake in the Outcome
d. Entrepreneur

35. In politics, a _________, (by metaphor with the carved _________ at the prow of a sailing ship), is a person who holds an important title or office yet executes little actual power, most commonly limited by convention rather than law. Common _________s include constitutional monarchs, such as: Queen Elizabeth II, the Emperor of Japan, or presidents in parliamentary democracies, such as the President of Israel.

While the authority of a _________ is in practice generally symbolic, public opinion, respect for the office or the office holder and access to high levels of government can give them significant influence on events.

a. 28-hour day
b. 1990 Clean Air Act
c. Figurehead
d. 33 Strategies of War

36. In finance, an _________ is a contract between a buyer and a seller that gives the buyer the right--but not the obligation--to buy or to sell a particular asset (the underlying asset) at a later day at an agreed price. In return for granting the _________, the seller collects a payment (the premium) from the buyer. A call _________ gives the buyer the right to buy the underlying asset; a put _________ gives the buyer of the _________ the right to sell the underlying asset.

a. AAAI
b. A4e
c. A Stake in the Outcome
d. Option

37. _________ is a pedagogical concept according to which newly acquired skills should be practiced well beyond the point of initial mastery, leading to automaticity.

The Yerkes-Dodson law predicts that _________ can improve performance in states of high arousal.

a. A Stake in the Outcome
b. A4e
c. AAAI
d. Overlearning

38. _________ refers to a range of skills, tools, and techniques used to manage time when accomplishing specific tasks, projects and goals. This set encompass a wide scope of activities, and these include planning, allocating, setting goals, delegation, analysis of time spent, monitoring, organizing, scheduling, and prioritizing. Initially _________ referred to just business or work activities, but eventually the term broadened to include personal activities also.

a. Voice of the customer
b. Time management
c. Cash cow
d. Formula for Change

39. The term '_________' refers to the concept of collecting information and attempting to spot a pattern in the information. In some fields of study, the term '_________' has more formally-defined meanings.

In project management _________ is a mathematical technique that uses historical results to predict future outcome.

a. Stepwise regression
b. Least squares
c. Regression analysis
d. Trend analysis

40. A chief executive officer (_________) or chief executive is one of the highest-ranking corporate officer (executive) or administrator in charge of total management. An individual selected as President and _________ of a corporation, company, organization, or agency, reports to the board of directors. In internal communication and press releases, many companies capitalize the term and those of other high positions, even when they are not proper nouns.

a. Director of communications
b. Portfolio manager
c. Chief executive officer
d. CEO

41. _________ according to Onuoha (2007) is the practice of starting new organizations or revitalizing mature organizations, particularly new businesses generally in response to identified opportunities. _________ is often a difficult undertaking, as a vast majority of new businesses fail. Entrepreneurial activities are substantially different depending on the type of organization that is being started.

a. AAAI
b. A4e
c. A Stake in the Outcome
d. Entrepreneurship

1. A _________ is the term given to a company that facilitates the learning of its members and continuously transforms itself. _________s develop as a result of the pressures facing modern organizations and enables them to remain competitive in the business environment. A _________ has five main features; systems thinking, personal mastery, mental models, shared vision and team learning.

a. Hoshin Kanri
b. Quality function deployment
c. 1990 Clean Air Act
d. Learning organization

2. _________ refers to bodies of techniques for investigating phenomena, acquiring new knowledge, or correcting and integrating previous knowledge. To be termed scientific, a method of inquiry must be based on gathering observable, empirical and measurable evidence subject to specific principles of reasoning. A _________ consists of the collection of data through observation and experimentation, and the formulation and testing of hypotheses.

a. 33 Strategies of War
b. 28-hour day
c. Scientific method
d. 1990 Clean Air Act

3. _________ is, in very basic words, a position a firm occupies against its competitors.

According to Michael Porter, the three methods for creating a sustainable _________ are through:

1. Cost leadership

2. Differentiation

3. Focus (economics)

a. 28-hour day
b. 1990 Clean Air Act
c. Theory Z
d. Competitive advantage

4. _________ is a theory of management that analyzes and synthesizes workflows, with the objective of improving labour productivity. The core ideas of the theory were developed by Frederick Winslow Taylor in the 1880s and 1890s, and were first published in his monographs, Shop Management and The Principles of _________ Taylor believed that decisions based upon tradition and rules of thumb should be replaced by precise procedures developed after careful study of an individual at work.

a. Value engineering
b. Capacity planning
c. Master production schedule
d. Scientific management

5. _________ is also known as operations management, management science, systems engineering, or manufacturing engineering; a distinction that seems to depend on the viewpoint or motives of the user. Recruiters or educational establishments use the names to differentiate themselves from others. In healthcare, for example, industrial engineers are more commonly known as management engineers or health systems engineers.

a. A Stake in the Outcome
b. AAAI
c. A4e
d. Industrial engineering

6. _________ or Behaviourism thinking and feeling--can and should be regarded as behaviors. The school of psychology maintains that behaviors as such can be described scientifically without recourse either to internal physiological events or to hypothetical constructs such as the mind. _________ comprises the position that all theories should have observational correlates but that there are no philosophical differences between publicly observable processes and privately observable processes

a. Psychometrics
b. Behaviorism
c. Cognitive dissonance
d. Borderline intellectual functioning

7. The _________ is a form of reactivity whereby subjects improve an aspect of their behavior being experimentally measured simply in response to the fact that they are being studied, not in response to any particular experimental manipulation.

The term was coined in 1955 by Henry A. Landsberger when analyzing older experiments from 1924-1932 at the Hawthorne Works (outside Chicago.) Hawthorne Works had commissioned a study to see if its workers would become more productive in higher or lower levels of light.

a. 33 Strategies of War
b. 1990 Clean Air Act
c. 28-hour day
d. Hawthorne effect

8. _________ Movement refers to those researchers of organizational development who study the behavior of people in groups, in particular workplace groups. It originated in the 1920s' Hawthorne studies, which examined the effects of social relations, motivation and employee satisfaction on factory productivity. The movement viewed workers in terms of their psychology and fit with companies, rather than as interchangeable parts.

a. Hersey-Blanchard situational theory
b. Work design
c. Participatory management
d. Human relations

9. _________ refers to those researchers of organizational development who study the behavior of people in groups, in particular workplace groups. It originated in the 1920s' Hawthorne studies, which examined the effects of social relations, motivation and employee satisfaction on factory productivity. The movement viewed workers in terms of their psychology and fit with companies, rather than as interchangeable parts.

a. Job analysis
b. Path-goal theory
c. Job satisfaction
d. Human relations movement

10. A _________ is a prediction that directly or indirectly causes itself to become true, by the very terms of the prophecy itself, due to positive feedback between belief and behavior. Although examples of such prophecies can be found in literature as far back as ancient Greece and ancient India, it is 20th-century sociologist Robert K. Merton who is credited with coining the expression '_________' and formalizing its structure and consequences. In his book Social Theory and Social Structure, Merton gives as a feature of the _________:

In other words, a prophecy declared as truth when it is actually false may sufficiently influence people, either through fear or logical confusion, so that their reactions ultimately fulfill the once-false prophecy.

a. 33 Strategies of War
b. Self-fulfilling prophecy
c. 1990 Clean Air Act
d. 28-hour day

11. Theory X and _________ are theories of human motivation created and developed by Douglas McGregor at the MIT Sloan School of Management in the 1960s that have been used in human resource management, organizational behavior, organizational communication and organizational development. They describe two very different attitudes toward workforce motivation. McGregor felt that companies followed either one or the other approach.

In _________, management assumes employees may be ambitious and self-motivated and exercise self-control. It is believed that employees enjoy their mental and physical work duties.

a. Contingency theory
b. Business Workflow Analysis
c. Design leadership
d. Theory Y

12. _________ can be regarded as an outcome of mental processes (cognitive process) leading to the selection of a course of action among several alternatives. Every _________ process produces a final choice. The output can be an action or an opinion of choice.

a. 33 Strategies of War
b. 28-hour day
c. Decision making
d. 1990 Clean Air Act

13. _________, is the discipline of using scientific research-based principles, strategies, and other analytical methods, such as mathematical modeling to improve any organization's ability to enact rational, meaningful business management decisions.

a. Management science
b. Cross ownership
c. Workflow
d. Trustee

14. _________ in the USA, Canada, South Africa and Australia, and operational research in Europe, is an interdisciplinary branch of applied mathematics and formal science that uses methods such as mathematical modeling, statistics, and algorithms to arrive at optimal or near optimal solutions to complex problems. It is typically concerned with optimizing the maxima (profit, assembly line performance, crop yield, bandwidth, etc) or minima (loss, risk, etc.) of some objective function.

a. A Stake in the Outcome
b. Operations research
c. AAAI
d. A4e

15. _________ is a structured approach to transitioning individuals, teams, and organizations from a current state to a desired future state. The current definition of _________ includes both organizational _________ processes and individual _________ models, which together are used to manage the people side of change.

A number of models are available for understanding the transitioning of individuals through the phases of _________ and strengthening organizational development initiative in both government and corporate sectors.

a. 28-hour day
b. Change management
c. 33 Strategies of War
d. 1990 Clean Air Act

16. _________ is an inventory strategy that strives to improve the return on investment of a business by reducing in-process inventory and its associated carrying costs. To meet _________ objectives, the process relies on signals between different points in the process. This means the process is often driven by a series of signals, or Kanban , which tell production when to make the next part. Kanban are usually 'tickets' but can be simple visual signals, such as the presence or absence of a part on a shelf. Implemented correctly, _________ can dramatically improve a manufacturing organization's return on investment, quality, and efficiency.

a. 1990 Clean Air Act
b. 33 Strategies of War
c. 28-hour day
d. Just-in-time

17. _________ is an area of business concerned with the production of goods and services, and involves the responsibility of ensuring that business operations are efficient in terms of using as little resource as needed, and effective in terms of meeting customer requirements. It is concerned with managing the process that converts inputs (in the forms of materials, labour and energy) into outputs (in the form of goods and services.)

Operations traditionally refers to the production of goods and services separately, although the distinction between these two main types of operations is increasingly difficult to make as manufacturers tend to merge product and service offerings.

a. AAAI
b. A Stake in the Outcome
c. Operations management
d. A4e

18. _________ is one of the managerial functions like planning, organizing, staffing and directing. It is an important function because it helps to check the errors and to take the corrective action so that deviation from standards are minimized and stated goals of the organization are achieved in desired manner.According to modern concepts, _________ is a foreseeing action whereas earlier concept of _________ was used only when errors were detected. _________ in management means setting standards, measuring actual performance and taking corrective action.

a. Control
b. Schedule of reinforcement
c. Turnover
d. Decision tree pruning

19. _________ refers to planned and systematic production processes that provide confidence in a product's suitability for its intended purpose. Refer to the definition by Merriam-Webster for further information . It is a set of activities intended to ensure that products (goods and/or services) satisfy customer requirements in a systematic, reliable fashion.

a. 1990 Clean Air Act
b. 28-hour day
c. Quality assurance
d. Risk assessment

20. In engineering and manufacturing, _________ and quality engineering are used in developing systems to ensure products or services are designed and produced to meet or exceed customer requirements. Refer to the definition by Merriam-Webster for further information . These systems are often developed in conjunction with other business and engineering disciplines using a cross-functional approach.

a. Statistical process control
b. Process capability
c. Single Minute Exchange of Die
d. Quality control

21. In management science, operations research and organizational development (OD), human organizations are viewed as systems (conceptual systems) of interacting components such as _________ or system aggregates, which are carriers of numerous complex processes and organizational structures. Organizational development theorist Peter Senge developed the notion of organizations as systems in his book The Fifth Discipline.

Systems thinking is a style of thinking/reasoning and problem solving.

a. 28-hour day
b. Systems thinking
c. 1990 Clean Air Act
d. Subsystems

22. _________ is a business management strategy aimed at embedding awareness of quality in all organizational processes. _________ has been widely used in manufacturing, education, hospitals, call centers, government, and service industries, as well as NASA space and science programs.

As defined by the International Organization for Standardization (ISO):

> '_________ is a management approach for an organization, centered on quality, based on the participation of all its members and aiming at long-term success through customer satisfaction, and benefits to all members of the organization and to society.' ISO 8402:1994

One major aim is to reduce variation from every process so that greater consistency of effort is obtained. (Royse, D., Thyer, B., Padgett D., ' Logan T., 2006)

a. Quality management
b. 1990 Clean Air Act
c. Total quality management
d. 28-hour day

23. _________ can be considered to have three main components: quality control, quality assurance and quality improvement. _________ is focused not only on product quality, but also the means to achieve it. _________ therefore uses quality assurance and control of processes as well as products to achieve more consistent quality.

a. 28-hour day
b. Quality management
c. Total quality management
d. 1990 Clean Air Act

24. _________ describes the situation when output from (or information about the result of) an event or phenomenon in the past will influence the same event/phenomenon in the present or future. When an event is part of a chain of cause-and-effect that forms a circuit or loop, then the event is said to 'feed back' into itself.

_________ is also a synonym for:

- _________ signal; the information about the initial event that is the basis for subsequent modification of the event.
- _________ loop; the causal path that leads from the initial generation of the _________ signal to the subsequent modification of the event.

_________ is a mechanism, process or signal that is looped back to control a system within itself. Such a loop is called a _________ loop.

a. 1990 Clean Air Act
b. Feedback loop
c. Positive feedback
d. Feedback

25. The term '_________' refers to the concept of collecting information and attempting to spot a pattern in the information. In some fields of study, the term '_________' has more formally-defined meanings.

In project management _________ is a mathematical technique that uses historical results to predict future outcome.

a. Trend analysis
b. Regression analysis
c. Stepwise regression
d. Least squares

26. _________ is a business magazine published by McGraw-Hill. It was first published in 1929 (as The Business Week) under the direction of Malcolm Muir, who was serving as president of the McGraw-Hill Publishing company at the time. Its primary competitors in the national business magazine category are Fortune and Forbes, which are published bi-weekly.

a. Hotel Vikas
b. Democracy in America
c. The Wealth of Nations
d. BusinessWeek

27. _________, commonly abbreviated to Gen X, is a term used to refer to a generational cohort of children born after the baby boom ended and usually prior to the 1980s

The term _________ has been used in demography, the social sciences, and marketing, though it is most often used in popular culture.

In the U.S. _________ was originally referred to as the 'baby bust' generation because of the drop in the birth rate following the baby boom.

a. Generation X
b. Affiliation
c. Abraham Harold Maslow
d. Adam Smith

28. _________ is a term used to describe the demographic cohort following Generation X. Its members are often referred to as 'Millennials' or 'Echo Boomers') . There are no precise dates for when Gen Y begins and ends. Most commentators use dates from the early 1980s to early 1990s.

a. Giovanni Agnelli
b. David Wittig
c. Benjamin R. Barber
d. Generation Y

29. A broad definition of _________ is the action of gathering, analyzing, and distributing information about products, customers, competitors and any aspect of the environment needed to support executives and managers in making strategic decisions for an organization.

Key points of this definitions:

1. _________ is an ethical and legal business practice. (This is important as _________ professionals emphasize that the discipline is not the same as industrial espionage which is both unethical and usually illegal.)
2. The focus is on the external business environment.
3. There is a process involved in gathering information, converting it into intelligence and then utilizing this in business decision making. _________ professionals emphasize that if the intelligence gathered is not usable (or actionable) then it is not intelligence.

A more focused definition of _________ regards it as the organizational function responsible for the early identification of risks and opportunities in the market before they become obvious. Experts also call this process the early signal analysis. This definition focuses attention on the difference between dissemination of widely available factual information (such as market statistics, financial reports, newspaper clippings) performed by functions such as libraries and information centers, and _________ which is a perspective on developments and events aimed at yielding a competitive edge.

a. 1990 Clean Air Act
b. Competitor or Competitive Intelligence
c. 28-hour day
d. Competitive intelligence

30. _________ refers to the process of screening, and selecting qualified people for a job at an organization or firm mid- and large-size organizations and companies often retain professional recruiters or outsource some of the process to _________ agencies. External _________ is the process of attracting and selecting employees from outside the organization.

The _________ industry has four main types of agencies: employment agencies, _________ websites and job search engines, 'headhunters' for executive and professional _________, and in-house _________.

a. Labour hire
b. Recruitment Process Outsourcing
c. Referral recruitment
d. Recruitment

31. _________ refers to metrics and measures of output from production processes, per unit of input. Labor _________, for example, is typically measured as a ratio of output per labor-hour, an input. _________ may be conceived of as a metrics of the technical or engineering efficiency of production.

a. Productivity
b. Remanufacturing
c. Value engineering
d. Master production schedule

32. _________ is a management technique pioneered by Michael Phillips in San Francisco in the late '60's and early '70s. The concept's most visible success was by Jack Stack and his team at SRC Holdings and popularized in 1995 by John Case. The technique is to give employees all relevant financial information about the company so they can make better decisions as workers.

a. A4e
b. Open-book management
c. AAAI
d. A Stake in the Outcome

33. The _________ captures an expanded spectrum of values and criteria for measuring organizational success: economic, ecological and social. With the ratification of the United Nations and ICLEI _________ standard for urban and community accounting in early 2007, this became the dominant approach to public sector full cost accounting. Similar UN standards apply to natural capital and human capital measurement to assist in measurements required by _________, e.g. the ecoBudget standard for reporting ecological footprint.

a. 33 Strategies of War
b. 28-hour day
c. 1990 Clean Air Act
d. Triple bottom line

34. _________ is an uncomfortable feeling caused by holding two contradictory ideas simultaneously. The 'ideas' or 'cognitions' in question may include attitudes and beliefs, and also the awareness of one's behavior. The theory of _________ proposes that people have a motivational drive to reduce dissonance by changing their attitudes, beliefs, and behaviors, or by justifying or rationalizing their attitudes, beliefs, and behaviors.

a. Quantitative psychology
b. Trait theory
c. Cognitive dissonance
d. Cognitive bias

35. _________ is a Japanese philosophy that focuses on continuous improvement throughout all aspects of life. When applied to the workplace, _________ activities continually improve all functions of a business, from manufacturing to management and from the CEO to the assembly line workers. By improving standardized activities and processes, _________ aims to eliminate waste .

a. Kaizen
b. Sensitivity analysis
c. Cross-docking
d. Psychological pricing

36. _________ is a term in psychology which refers to a person's belief about what causes the good or bad results in his or her life, either in general or in a specific area such as health or academics. Understanding of the concept was developed by Julian B. Rotter in 1954, and has since become an important aspect of personality studies.

_________ refers to the extent to which individuals believe that they can control events that affect them.

a. Machiavellianism
b. Social loafing
c. Self-enhancement
d. Locus of control

37. In psychology, _________ reflects a person's overall evaluation or appraisal of his or her own worth.

_________ encompasses beliefs (for example, 'I am competent/incompetent') and emotions (for example, triumph/despair, pride/shame.) Behavior may reflect _________

a. 1990 Clean Air Act
b. Self-esteem
c. 33 Strategies of War
d. 28-hour day

38. In the social psychology of groups, _________ is the phenomenon of people making less effort to achieve a goal when they work in a group than when they work alone. This is seen as one of the main reasons groups are sometimes less productive than the combined performance of their members working as individuals.

- Ringelmann, Max : 1913

Research began in 1913 with Max Ringelmann's study. He found that when he asked a group of men to pull on a rope, that they did not pull as hard, or put as much effort into the activity, as they did when they were pulling alone.

a. Self-enhancement
b. Personal space
c. Machiavellianism
d. Social loafing

39. The term _________ refers to a salaried professional or an educated worker who performs semi-professional office, administrative, and sales coordination tasks, as opposed to a blue-collar worker, whose job requires manual labor. 'White-collar work' is an informal term, defined in contrast to 'blue-collar work'.

The term 'white collar' was first used by Upton Sinclair in relation to modern clerical, administrative and management workers during the 1930s.

a. 33 Strategies of War
b. 28-hour day
c. 1990 Clean Air Act
d. White-collar worker

1. _________ is a concept in ethics with several meanings. It is often used synonymously with such concepts as responsibility, answerability, enforcement, blameworthiness, liability and other terms associated with the expectation of account-giving. As an aspect of governance, it has been central to discussions related to problems in both the public and private (corporation) worlds.

a. Usury
b. A Stake in the Outcome
c. Accountability
d. A4e

2. _________ refers to the long-term management of intractable conflicts. It is the label for the variety of ways by which people handle grievances--standing up for what they consider to be right and against what they consider to be wrong. Those ways include such diverse phenomena as gossip, ridicule, lynching, terrorism, warfare, feuding, genocide, law, mediation, and avoidance.

a. Conflict management
b. 1990 Clean Air Act
c. 33 Strategies of War
d. 28-hour day

3. A _________ is a body of elected or appointed members who jointly oversee the activities of a company or organization. The body sometimes has a different name, such as board of trustees, board of governors, board of managers, or executive board. It is often simply referred to as 'the board.'

A board's activities are determined by the powers, duties, and responsibilities delegated to it or conferred on it by an authority outside itself.

a. Foreign Corrupt Practices Act
b. Clean Water Act
c. Competition law
d. Board of directors

4. The 'business case for _________', theorizes that in a global marketplace, a company that employs a diverse workforce (both men and women, people of many generations, people from ethnically and racially diverse backgrounds etc.) is better able to understand the demographics of the marketplace it serves and is thus better equipped to thrive in that marketplace than a company that has a more limited range of employee demographics.

An additional corollary suggests that a company that supports the _________ of its workforce can also improve employee satisfaction, productivity and retention.

a. Diversity
b. Trademark
c. Virtual team
d. Kanban

5. _________ is the state or fact of exclusive rights and control over property, which may be an object, land/real estate or intellectual property. An _________ right is also referred to as title. The concept of _________ has existed for thousands of years and in all cultures.

a. A4e
b. A Stake in the Outcome
c. Emanation of the state
d. Ownership

6. A _________ is a type of business entity in which partners (owners) share with each other the profits or losses of the business. _________s are often favored over corporations for taxation purposes, as the _________ structure does not generally incur a tax on profits before it is distributed to the partners (i.e. there is no dividend tax levied.) However, depending on the _________ structure and the jurisdiction in which it operates, owners of a _________ may be exposed to greater personal liability than they would as shareholders of a corporation.

a. Partnership
b. Federal Employers Liability Act
c. Mediation
d. Due process

7. Contingency leadership theory in organizational studies is a type of leadership theory, leadership style, and leadership model that presumes that different leadership styles are contingent to different situations. It is also referred as _________ Â® theory although, as originally convened, the situational theory term is much more restrictive. The original situational theory argues that the best type of leadership is totally determined by the situational variables.Currently there are many styles of leadership.

a. Situational leadership
b. 28-hour day
c. Situational theory
d. 1990 Clean Air Act

8. A mutual shareholder or _________ is an individual or company (including a corporation) that legally owns one or more shares of stock in a joint stock company. A company's shareholders collectively own that company. Thus, the typical goal of such companies is to enhance shareholder value.

a. Free riding
b. Shareholder
c. 1990 Clean Air Act
d. Stockholder

9. _________ has been described as the 'process of social influence in which one person can enlist the aid and support of others in the accomplishment of a common task' . A definition more inclusive of followers comes from Alan Keith of Genentech who said '_________ is ultimately about creating a way for people to contribute to making something extraordinary happen.'

_________ is one of the most salient aspects of the organizational context. However, defining _________ has been challenging.

a. 1990 Clean Air Act
b. Situational leadership
c. 28-hour day
d. Leadership

10. _________ is a legal term that refers to a holder of property on behalf of a beneficiary. A trust can be set up either to benefit particular persons, or for any charitable purposes (but not generally for non-charitable purposes): typical examples are a will trust for the testator's children and family, a pension trust (to confer benefits on employees and their families), and a charitable trust. In all cases, the _________ may be a person or company, whether or not they are a prospective beneficiary.

a. Commercial management
b. Trustee
c. Design management
d. Hierarchical organization

11. _________ is a term defined by the Oxford English Dictionary as an individual's 'course or progress through life '. It is usually considered to pertain to remunerative work (and sometimes also formal education.)

The etymology of the term is somewhat ironic in that it comes from the Latin word carrera, which means race .

a. Career planning
b. Spatial mismatch
c. Nursing shortage
d. Career

12. The _________ captures an expanded spectrum of values and criteria for measuring organizational success: economic, ecological and social. With the ratification of the United Nations and ICLEI _________ standard for urban and community accounting in early 2007, this became the dominant approach to public sector full cost accounting. Similar UN standards apply to natural capital and human capital measurement to assist in measurements required by _________, e.g. the ecoBudget standard for reporting ecological footprint.

a. 28-hour day
b. 33 Strategies of War
c. 1990 Clean Air Act
d. Triple bottom line

13. _________ is a term coined by Deborah E. Meyerson used to describe corporate professionals who work toward positive change in both their work environment and the way their companies conduct business -- often taking 'radical' action that is just short of getting them fired.

In her book, _________: How Everyday Leaders Inspire Change at Work (Harvard Business School Press), Meyerson describes employees who believe and work toward creating adaptive, family-friendly, and socially responsible workplaces.

_________ are quiet leaders that act as catalysts for new ideas, alternative perspectives, and organizational learning and change -- and balance company conformity with individual rebellion.

a. 28-hour day
b. 1990 Clean Air Act
c. 33 Strategies of War
d. Tempered Radicals

14. The _________ is an agency of the United States Department of Health and Human Services and is responsible for regulating and supervising the safety of foods, dietary supplements, drugs, vaccines, biological medical products, blood products, medical devices, radiation-emitting devices, veterinary products, and cosmetics. The FDA also enforces section 361 of the Public Health Service Act and the associated regulations, including sanitation requirements on interstate travel as well as specific rules for control of disease on products ranging from pet turtles to semen donations for assisted reproductive medicine techniques.

The FDA is an agency within the United States Department of Health and Human Services responsible for protecting and promoting the nation's public health.

a. 1990 Clean Air Act
b. 28-hour day
c. Food and Drug Administration
d. 33 Strategies of War

15. The act of becoming a surety is also called a _________. Traditionally a _________ was distinguished from a surety in that the surety's liability was joint and primary with the principal, whereas the guaranty's liability was ancillary and derivative, but many jurisdictions have abolished this distinction

a. Guarantee
b. National treatment
c. Clayton Antitrust Act
d. Blue sky law

16. A _________ or labor union is an organization of workers who have banded together to achieve common goals in key areas and working conditions. The _________, through its leadership, bargains with the employer on behalf of union members (rank and file members) and negotiates labor contracts (Collective bargaining) with employers. This may include the negotiation of wages, work rules, complaint procedures, rules governing hiring, firing and promotion of workers, benefits, workplace safety and policies.

a. Working time
b. Company union
c. Labour law
d. Trade union

17. A _________ is a relatively new executive level position at a corporation, company, organization typically reporting directly to the CEO or board of directors. The _________ is responsible for a brand's image, experience, and promise, and propagating it throughout all aspects of the company. The brand officer oversees marketing, advertising, design, public relations and customer service departments.

a. Director of communications
b. Purchasing manager
c. Chief executive officer
d. Chief brand officer

18. _________ or _________ data refers to selected population characteristics as used in government, marketing or opinion research, or the _________ profiles used in such research. Note the distinction from the term 'demography' Commonly-used _________s include race, age, income, disabilities, mobility (in terms of travel time to work or number of vehicles available), educational attainment, home ownership, employment status, and even location.

a. Adam Smith
b. Demographic
c. Abraham Harold Maslow
d. Affiliation

19. The _________ of 1990 (ADA) is the short title of United States (Pub.L. 101-336, 104 Stat. 327, enacted July 26, 1990), codified at 42 U.S.C. Â§ 12101 et seq. It was signed into law on July 26, 1990, by President George H. W. Bush, and later amended with changes effective January 1, 2009. The ADA is a wide-ranging civil rights law that prohibits, under certain circumstances, discrimination based on disability. It affords similar protections against discrimination to Americans with disabilities as the Civil Rights Act of 1964,

a. Australian labour law
b. Americans with Disabilities Act
c. Employment discrimination
d. Equal Pay Act of 1963

20. An _________ is a situation that will often involve an apparent conflict between moral imperatives, in which to obey one would result in transgressing another. This is also called an ethical paradox since in moral philosophy, paradox plays a central role in ethics debates. For instance, an ethical admonition to 'love thy neighbour as thy self' is not always just in contrast with, but sometimes in contradiction to an armed neighbour actively trying to kill you: if he or she succeeds, you will not be able to love him or her.

a. A4e
b. AAAI
c. A Stake in the Outcome
d. Ethical dilemma

21. A _________ is a set of consistent ethic values (more specifically the personal and cultural values) and measures used for the purpose of ethical or ideological integrity. A well defined _________ is a moral code.

Fred Wenst>øp and Arild Myrmel have proposed a structure for corporate _________s that consists of three value categories. These are considered complementary and juxtaposed on the same level if illustrated graphically on for instance an organization's web page. The first value category is Core Values, which prescribe the attitude and character of an organization, and are often found in sections on Code of conduct on its web page. The philosophical antecedents of these values are Virtue ethics, which is often attributed to Aristotle. Protected Values are protected through rules, standards and certifications. They are often concerned with areas such as health, environment and safety. The third category, Created Values, is the values that stakeholders, including the shareholders expect in return for their contributions to the firm. These values are subject to trade-off by decision-makers or bargaining processes. This process is explained further in Stakeholder theory.

a. 1990 Clean Air Act
b. 28-hour day
c. 33 Strategies of War
d. Value system

22. _________ is a term that refers both to:

- a formal discipline used to help appraise, or assess, the case for a project or proposal, which itself is a process known as project appraisal; and
- an informal approach to making decisions of any kind.

Under both definitions the process involves, whether explicitly or implicitly, weighing the total expected costs against the total expected benefits of one or more actions in order to choose the best or most profitable option. The formal process is often referred to as either CBA (_________) or BCost-benefit analysis

A hallmark of CBA is that all benefits and all costs are expressed in money terms, and are adjusted for the time value of money, so that all flows of benefits and flows of project costs over time (which tend to occur at different points in time) are expressed on a common basis in terms of their 'present value.' Closely related, but slightly different, formal techniques include Cost-effectiveness analysis, Economic impact analysis, Fiscal impact analysis and Social Return on Investment(SROI) analysis. The latter builds upon the logic of _________, but differs in that it is explicitly designed to inform the practical decision-making of enterprise managers and investors focused on optimising their social and environmental impacts.

a. Kepner-Tregoe
b. Cost-benefit analysis
c. Gittins index
d. Decision engineering

23. A _________ is a person who alleges misconduct. More complex definitions may be used, but the issue is that the _________ usually faces reprisal. The misconduct may be classified in many ways; for example, a violation of a law, rule, regulation and/or a direct threat to public interest, such as fraud, health/safety violations, and corruption.

a. Whistleblower
b. 33 Strategies of War
c. 1990 Clean Air Act
d. 28-hour day

24. _________, commonly abbreviated to Gen X, is a term used to refer to a generational cohort of children born after the baby boom ended and usually prior to the 1980s

The term _________ has been used in demography, the social sciences, and marketing, though it is most often used in popular culture.

In the U.S. _________ was originally referred to as the 'baby bust' generation because of the drop in the birth rate following the baby boom.

a. Abraham Harold Maslow
b. Affiliation
c. Adam Smith
d. Generation X

25. In economics, the term _________ refers to situations where the advancement of a qualified person within the hierarchy of an organization is stopped at a lower level because of some form of discrimination, most commonly sexism or racism, but since the term was coined, '_________' has also come to describe the limited advancement of the deaf, blind, disabled, aged and sexual minorities.It is an unofficial, invisible barrier that prevents women and minorities from advancing in businesses.

This situation is referred to as a 'ceiling' as there is a limitation blocking upward advancement, and 'glass' (transparent) because the limitation is not immediately apparent and is normally an unwritten and unofficial policy. This invisible barrier continues to exist, even though there are no explicit obstacles keeping minorities from acquiring advanced job positions - there are no advertisements that specifically say 'no minorities hired at this establishment', nor are there any formal orders that say 'minorities are not qualified' - but they do lie beneath the surface.

a. 1990 Clean Air Act
b. 28-hour day
c. 33 Strategies of War
d. Glass ceiling

26. The term '_________' refers to the concept of collecting information and attempting to spot a pattern in the information. In some fields of study, the term '_________' has more formally-defined meanings.

In project management _________ is a mathematical technique that uses historical results to predict future outcome.

a. Stepwise regression
b. Regression analysis
c. Least squares
d. Trend analysis

27. The _________ is the labour pool in employment. It is generally used to describe those working for a single company or industry, but can also apply to a geographic region like a city, country, state, etc. The term generally excludes the employers or management, and implies those involved in manual labour.

a. Pink-collar worker
b. Work-life balance
c. Division of labour
d. Workforce

28. In economics, the term _________ has three different distinct meanings and applications. While it is related to unemployment, a situation in which a person who is searching for work cannot find a job, in the case of _________, a person is working. All three of the definitions of '_________' involve underutilization of labor that critics say is missed by most official (governmental agency) definitions and measurements of unemployment.

a. Underemployment
b. Employee handbook
c. Occupational Employment Statistics
d. Encore career

29. _________ is, in its simplest form, the practice of favoring members of a historically disadvantaged group at the expense of members of a historically advantaged group.

In the United States, the terms '_________' and 'reverse racism' have been used in past discussions of racial quotas or gender quotas for collegiate admission to government-run educational institutions. Such policies were held to be unconstitutional in the United States, while non-quota race preferences are legal.

a. Sexism,
b. Separate but equal
c. Reverse discrimination
d. 1990 Clean Air Act

30. In economics, _________ is the desire to own something and the ability to pay for it. The term _________ signifies the ability or the willingness to buy a particular commodity at a given point of time.

a. Demand
b. 1990 Clean Air Act
c. 33 Strategies of War
d. 28-hour day

31. _________ is the strategic and coherent approach to the management of an organisation's most valued assets - the people working there who individually and collectively contribute to the achievement of the objectives of the business. The terms '_________' and 'human resources' (HR) have largely replaced the term 'personnel management' as a description of the processes involved in managing people in organizations. In simple sense, _________ means employing people, developing their resources, utilizing, maintaining and compensating their services in tune with the job and organizational requirement.

a. Job knowledge
b. Progressive discipline
c. Revolving door syndrome
d. Human resource management

32. _________ according to Onuoha (2007) is the practice of starting new organizations or revitalizing mature organizations, particularly new businesses generally in response to identified opportunities. _________ is often a difficult undertaking, as a vast majority of new businesses fail. Entrepreneurial activities are substantially different depending on the type of organization that is being started.

a. Entrepreneurship
b. AAAI
c. A4e
d. A Stake in the Outcome

33. An _________ is a person who has possession of an enterprise and assumes significant accountability for the inherent risks and the outcome. It is an ambitious leader who combines land, labor, and capital to create and market new goods or services. The term is a loanword from French and was first defined by the Irish economist Richard Cantillon.

a. AAAI
b. A4e
c. A Stake in the Outcome
d. Entrepreneur

34. _________ is a term in psychology which refers to a person's belief about what causes the good or bad results in his or her life, either in general or in a specific area such as health or academics. Understanding of the concept was developed by Julian B. Rotter in 1954, and has since become an important aspect of personality studies.

_________ refers to the extent to which individuals believe that they can control events that affect them.

a. Social loafing
b. Self-enhancement
c. Machiavellianism
d. Locus of control

35. _________ is a variable work schedule, in contrast to traditional work arrangements requiring employees to work a standard 9am to 5pm day. Under _________, there is typically a core period of the day when employees are expected to be at work (for example, between 11 am and 3pm), while the rest of the working day is 'flexitime', in which employees can choose when they work, subject to achieving total daily, weekly or monthly hours in the region of what the employer expects, and subject to the necessary work being done.

A _________ policy allows staff to determine when they will work, while a flexplace policy allows staff to determine where they will work.

a. Bennett Amendment
b. Flextime
c. Certificate of Incorporation
d. Fiduciary

36. _________ is a mathematical science pertaining to the collection, analysis, interpretation or explanation, and presentation of data. It also provides tools for prediction and forecasting based on data. It is applicable to a wide variety of academic disciplines, from the natural and social sciences to the humanities, government and business.

a. Location parameter
b. Simple moving average
c. Failure rate
d. Statistics

37. _________ generally refers to a list of all planned expenses and revenues. It is a plan for saving and spending. A _________ is an important concept in microeconomics, which uses a _________ line to illustrate the trade-offs between two or more goods.

a. 33 Strategies of War
b. Budget
c. 1990 Clean Air Act
d. 28-hour day

38. _________ is one of the managerial functions like planning, organizing, staffing and directing. It is an important function because it helps to check the errors and to take the corrective action so that deviation from standards are minimized and stated goals of the organization are achieved in desired manner.According to modern concepts, _________ is a foreseeing action whereas earlier concept of _________ was used only when errors were detected. _________ in management means setting standards, measuring actual performance and taking corrective action.

a. Control
b. Decision tree pruning
c. Schedule of reinforcement
d. Turnover

39. _________ can be regarded as an outcome of mental processes (cognitive process) leading to the selection of a course of action among several alternatives. Every _________ process produces a final choice. The output can be an action or an opinion of choice.

a. 33 Strategies of War
b. 28-hour day
c. 1990 Clean Air Act
d. Decision making

40. An _________ is a person temporarily or permanently residing in a country and culture other than that of the person's upbringing or legal residence. The word comes from the Latin ex and patria (country, fatherland.)

The term is sometimes used in the context of Westerners living in non-Western countries, although it is also used to describe Westerners living in other Western countries, such as Americans living in the United Kingdom, or Britons living in Spain.

a. A4e
b. A Stake in the Outcome
c. AAAI
d. Expatriate

41. Engineering _________ is the permissible limit of variation in

1. a physical dimension,
2. a measured value or physical property of a material, manufactured object, system, or service,
3. other measured values (such as temperature, humidity, etc.)
4. in engineering and safety, a physical distance or space (_________), as in a truck (lorry), train or boat under a bridge as well as a train in a tunnel

Dimensions, properties, or conditions may vary within certain practical limits without significantly affecting functioning of equipment or a process. _________s are specified to allow reasonable leeway for imperfections and inherent variability without compromising performance.

The _________ may be specified as a factor or percentage of the nominal value, a maximum deviation from a nominal value, an explicit range of allowed values, be specified by a note or published standard with this information, or be implied by the numeric accuracy of the nominal value. _________ can be symmetrical, as in 40±0.1, or asymmetrical, such as 40+0.2/−0.1.

a. Root cause analysis
b. Zero defects
c. Quality assurance
d. Tolerance

42. _________ occurs when a corporation is owned in whole or in part by its employees. Employees are usually given a share of the corporation after a certain length of employment or they can buy shares at any time. A corporation owned entirely by its employees (such as a worker cooperative) will not, therefore, have its shares sold on public stock markets, often opting instead for mixed ownership arrangements involving a trust.

a. Anaconda Copper
b. Amoco Corporation
c. AT'T Inc.
d. Employee Ownership

43. _________ is an uncomfortable feeling caused by holding two contradictory ideas simultaneously. The 'ideas' or 'cognitions' in question may include attitudes and beliefs, and also the awareness of one's behavior. The theory of _________ proposes that people have a motivational drive to reduce dissonance by changing their attitudes, beliefs, and behaviors, or by justifying or rationalizing their attitudes, beliefs, and behaviors.

a. Cognitive bias
b. Quantitative psychology
c. Trait theory
d. Cognitive dissonance

44. A _________ is a list of the general tasks and responsibilities of a position. Typically, it also includes to whom the position reports, specifications such as the qualifications needed by the person in the job, salary range for the position, etc. A _________ is usually developed by conducting a job analysis, which includes examining the tasks and sequences of tasks necessary to perform the job.

a. Recruitment advertising
b. Job description
c. Recruitment
d. Recruitment Process Insourcing

45. _________ Movement refers to those researchers of organizational development who study the behavior of people in groups, in particular workplace groups. It originated in the 1920s' Hawthorne studies, which examined the effects of social relations, motivation and employee satisfaction on factory productivity. The movement viewed workers in terms of their psychology and fit with companies, rather than as interchangeable parts.

a. Hersey-Blanchard situational theory
b. Work design
c. Participatory management
d. Human relations

46. _________ is about the mental processes regarding choice, or choosing. It explains the processes that an individual undergoes to make choices. In organizational behavior study, _________ is a motivation theory first proposed by Victor Vroom of the Yale School of Management.

a. A Stake in the Outcome
b. Expectancy theory
c. AAAI
d. A4e

47. _________, e-commuting, e-work, telework, working from home (WFH), or working at home (WAH) is a work arrangement in which employees enjoy flexibility in working location and hours. In other words, the daily commute to a central place of work is replaced by telecommunication links. Many work from home, while others, occasionally also referred to as nomad workers or web commuters utilize mobile telecommunications technology to work from coffee shops or myriad other locations.

a. Telecommuting
b. 1990 Clean Air Act
c. 28-hour day
d. 33 Strategies of War

1. _________ in its literal sense is the process of transformation of local or regional phenomena into global ones. It can be described as a process by which the people of the world are unified into a single society and function together.

This process is a combination of economic, technological, sociocultural and political forces.

a. Cost Management
b. Histogram
c. Collaborative Planning, Forecasting and Replenishment
d. Globalization

2. _________ generally refers to a list of all planned expenses and revenues. It is a plan for saving and spending. A _________ is an important concept in microeconomics, which uses a _________ line to illustrate the trade-offs between two or more goods.

a. 33 Strategies of War
b. 28-hour day
c. 1990 Clean Air Act
d. Budget

3. _________ Movement refers to those researchers of organizational development who study the behavior of people in groups, in particular workplace groups. It originated in the 1920s' Hawthorne studies, which examined the effects of social relations, motivation and employee satisfaction on factory productivity. The movement viewed workers in terms of their psychology and fit with companies, rather than as interchangeable parts.

a. Participatory management
b. Human relations
c. Work design
d. Hersey-Blanchard situational theory

4. _________ refers to those researchers of organizational development who study the behavior of people in groups, in particular workplace groups. It originated in the 1920s' Hawthorne studies, which examined the effects of social relations, motivation and employee satisfaction on factory productivity. The movement viewed workers in terms of their psychology and fit with companies, rather than as interchangeable parts.

a. Job satisfaction
b. Job analysis
c. Path-goal theory
d. Human relations movement

5. _________ is the strategic and coherent approach to the management of an organisation's most valued assets - the people working there who individually and collectively contribute to the achievement of the objectives of the business. The terms '_________' and 'human resources' (HR) have largely replaced the term 'personnel management' as a description of the processes involved in managing people in organizations. In simple sense, _________ means employing people, developing their resources, utilizing, maintaining and compensating their services in tune with the job and organizational requirement.

a. Job knowledge
b. Revolving door syndrome
c. Human resource management
d. Progressive discipline

6. An _________ is a practitioner of accountancy, which is the measurement, disclosure or provision of assurance about financial information that helps managers, investors, tax authorities and other decision makers make resource allocation decisions.

The word '_________' is derived from the French 'Compter' which took its origin from the Latin 'Computare'. The word was formerly written in English as 'Accomptant', but in process of time the word, which was always pronounced by dropping the 'p', became gradually changed both in pronunciation and in orthography to its present form.

a. A4e
b. A Stake in the Outcome
c. AAAI
d. Accountant

7. _________, commonly known as e-commerce, consists of the buying and selling of products or services over electronic systems such as the Internet and other computer networks. The amount of trade conducted electronically has grown extraordinarily with widespread Internet usage. The use of commerce is conducted in this way, spurring and drawing on innovations in electronic funds transfer, supply chain management, Internet marketing, online transaction processing, electronic data interchange (EDI), inventory management systems, and automated data collection systems.

a. Electronic Commerce
b. A4e
c. Online shopping
d. A Stake in the Outcome

8. _________ is the branch of economics that studies the dynamics of exchange rates, foreign investment, and how these affect international trade. It also studies international projects, international investments and capital flows, and trade deficits. It includes the study of futures, options and currency swaps.

a. International finance
b. A4e
c. A Stake in the Outcome
d. AAAI

9. A _________ -- also known as a geographically dispersed team -- is a group of individuals who work across time, space, and organizational boundaries with links strengthened by webs of communication technology. They have complementary skills and are committed to a common purpose, have interdependent performance goals, and share an approach to work for which they hold themselves mutually accountable. Geographically dispersed teams allow organizations to hire and retain the best people regardless of location.

a. Kanban
b. Trademark
c. Risk management
d. Virtual team

10. _________, commonly referred to as 'eBusiness' or 'e-Business', may be defined as the utilization of information and communication technologies (ICT) in support of all the activities of business. Commerce constitutes the exchange of products and services between businesses, groups and individuals and hence can be seen as one of the essential activities of any business. Hence, electronic commerce or eCommerce focuses on the use of ICT to enable the external activities and relationships of the business with individuals, groups and other businesses .

a. Electronic business
b. A Stake in the Outcome
c. AAAI
d. A4e

11. _________ is a term defined by the Oxford English Dictionary as an individual's 'course or progress through life '. It is usually considered to pertain to remunerative work (and sometimes also formal education.)

The etymology of the term is somewhat ironic in that it comes from the Latin word carrera, which means race .

a. Nursing shortage
b. Career planning
c. Spatial mismatch
d. Career

12. _________ is a reduction in the value of a currency with respect to other monetary units. In common modern usage, it specifically implies an official lowering of the value of a country's currency within a fixed exchange rate system, by which the monetary authority formally sets a new fixed rate with respect to a foreign reference currency. In contrast, depreciation is used for the unofficial decrease in the exchange rate in a floating exchange rate system.

a. Devaluation
b. 1990 Clean Air Act
c. 33 Strategies of War
d. 28-hour day

13. _________ has been described as the 'process of social influence in which one person can enlist the aid and support of others in the accomplishment of a common task' . A definition more inclusive of followers comes from Alan Keith of Genentech who said '_________ is ultimately about creating a way for people to contribute to making something extraordinary happen.'

_________ is one of the most salient aspects of the organizational context. However, defining _________ has been challenging.

a. 1990 Clean Air Act
b. Situational leadership
c. 28-hour day
d. Leadership

14. _________ comprises a range of practices used in an organisation to identify, create, represent, distribute and enable adoption of insights and experiences. Such insights and experiences comprise knowledge, either embodied in individuals or embedded in organisational processes or practice.

An established discipline since 1991 , _________ includes courses taught in the fields of business administration, information systems, management, and library and information sciences .

a. 1990 Clean Air Act
b. 28-hour day
c. 33 Strategies of War
d. Knowledge management

15. A _________ in today's workforce is an individual that is valued for their ability to interpret information within a specific subject area. They will often advance the overall understanding of that subject through focused analysis, design and/or development. They use research skills to define problems and to identify alternatives.

a. Knowledge worker
b. Career development
c. Customer satisfaction
d. Business rule

16. A _________ or transnational corporation is a corporation or enterprise that manages production or delivers services in more than one country. It can also be referred to as an international corporation.

The first modern _________ is generally thought to be the Dutch East India Company, established in 1602.

a. Command center
b. Multinational corporation
c. Financial Accounting Standards Board
d. Small and medium enterprises

17. _________ is exchange of capital, goods, and services across international borders or territories. In most countries, it represents a significant share of gross domestic product (GDP.) While _________ has been present throughout much of history , its economic, social, and political importance has been on the rise in recent centuries.

a. A4e
b. AAAI
c. International trade
d. A Stake in the Outcome

18. A _________ is a process in which a potential employee is evaluated by an employer for prospective employment in their company, organization and was established in the late 16th century.

A _________ typically precedes the hiring decision, and is used to evaluate the candidate. The interview is usually preceded by the evaluation of submitted résumés from interested candidates, then selecting a small number of candidates for interviews.

a. Supported employment
b. Split shift
c. Payrolling
d. Job interview

19. An _________ is a person temporarily or permanently residing in a country and culture other than that of the person's upbringing or legal residence. The word comes from the Latin ex and patria (country, fatherland.)

The term is sometimes used in the context of Westerners living in non-Western countries, although it is also used to describe Westerners living in other Western countries, such as Americans living in the United Kingdom, or Britons living in Spain.

a. AAAI
b. A Stake in the Outcome
c. Expatriate
d. A4e

20. A _________ is an entity formed between two or more parties to undertake economic activity together. The parties agree to create a new entity by both contributing equity, and they then share in the revenues, expenses, and control of the enterprise. The venture can be for one specific project only, or a continuing business relationship such as the Fuji Xerox _________.

a. Joint venture
b. Meritor Savings Bank v. Vinson
c. Civil Rights Act of 1991
d. Patent

21. The _________ is the Cabinet department of the United States government concerned with promoting economic growth. It was originally created as the _________ and Labor on February 14, 1903. It was subsequently renamed to the Department of Commerce on March 4, 1913, and its bureaus and agencies specializing in labor were transferred to the new Department of Labor.

a. AAAI
b. A4e
c. A Stake in the Outcome
d. United States Department of Commerce

22. An _________ is a person who has possession of an enterprise and assumes significant accountability for the inherent risks and the outcome. It is an ambitious leader who combines land, labor, and capital to create and market new goods or services. The term is a loanword from French and was first defined by the Irish economist Richard Cantillon.

a. A4e
b. Entrepreneur
c. A Stake in the Outcome
d. AAAI

23. A _________ or maquila is a factory that imports materials and equipment on a duty-free and tariff-free basis for assembly or manufacturing and then re-exports the assembled product, usually back to the originating country. A maquila is also referred to as a 'twin plant', or 'in-bond' industry. Nearly half a million Mexicans are employed in _________s.

a. 33 Strategies of War
b. Maquiladora
c. 28-hour day
d. 1990 Clean Air Act

24. _________ Management is the succession of strategies used by management as a product goes through its _________. The conditions in which a product is sold changes over time and must be managed as it moves through its succession of stages.

The _________ goes through many phases, involves many professional disciplines, and requires many skills, tools and processes.

a. Strategic Alliance
b. Golden handshake
c. Product life cycle
d. Job hunting

25. _________ describes the relocation by a company of a business process from one country to another -- typically an operational process, such as manufacturing such as accounting. Even state governments employ _________.

The term is in use in several distinct but closely related ways.

a. AAAI
b. A4e
c. Offshoring
d. A Stake in the Outcome

26. _________ is subcontracting a process, such as product design or manufacturing, to a third-party company. The decision to outsource is often made in the interest of lowering cost or making better use of time and energy costs, redirecting or conserving energy directed at the competencies of a particular business, or to make more efficient use of land, labor, capital, (information) technology and resources. _________ became part of the business lexicon during the 1980s.

a. Unemployment insurance
b. Outsourcing
c. Operant conditioning
d. Opinion leadership

27. _________ is a sub-topic of machine learning. It is 'the act of taking in raw data and taking an action based on the category of the data'. Most research in _________ is about methods for supervised learning and unsupervised learning.

a. 1990 Clean Air Act
b. 28-hour day
c. 33 Strategies of War
d. Pattern recognition

28. _________ is a mathematical science pertaining to the collection, analysis, interpretation or explanation, and presentation of data. It also provides tools for prediction and forecasting based on data. It is applicable to a wide variety of academic disciplines, from the natural and social sciences to the humanities, government and business.

a. Simple moving average
b. Location parameter
c. Failure rate
d. Statistics

29. _________ refers to the methods of practicing and using another person's business philosophy. The franchisor grants the independent operator the right to distribute its products, techniques, and trademarks for a percentage of gross monthly sales and a royalty fee. Various tangibles and intangibles such as national or international advertising, training, and other support services are commonly made available by the franchisor.

a. 28-hour day
b. 1990 Clean Air Act
c. ServiceMaster
d. Franchising

30. A _________ is a formal relationship between two or more parties to pursue a set of agreed upon goals or to meet a critical business need while remaining independent organizations.

Partners may provide the _________ with resources such as products, distribution channels, manufacturing capability, project funding, capital equipment, knowledge, expertise, or intellectual property. The alliance is a cooperation or collaboration which aims for a synergy where each partner hopes that the benefits from the alliance will be greater than those from individual efforts.

a. Process automation
b. Strategic alliance
c. Farmshoring
d. Golden parachute

31. A _________, in business matters, is an entity that is controlled by a bigger and more powerful entity. The controlled entity is called a company, corporation, or limited liability company and in some cases can be a government or state-owned enterprise, and the controlling entity is called its parent (or the parent company.) The reason for this distinction is that a lone company cannot be a _________ of any organization; only an entity representing a legal fiction as a separate entity can be a _________.

a. 33 Strategies of War
b. 1990 Clean Air Act
c. 28-hour day
d. Subsidiary

32. _________ is the incidence or process of transferring ownership of a business, enterprise, agency or public service from the public sector (government) to the private sector (business.) In a broader sense, _________ refers to transfer of any government function to the private sector including governmental functions like revenue collection and law enforcement.

a. Privatization
b. 28-hour day
c. Performance reports
d. 1990 Clean Air Act

33. In finance, the _________s between two currencies specifies how much one currency is worth in terms of the other. It is the value of a foreign nation's currency in terms of the home nation's currency. For example an _________ of 102 Japanese yen to the United States dollar means that JPY 102 is worth the same as USD 1.

a. AAAI
b. A Stake in the Outcome
c. Exchange rate
d. A4e

34. _________ is a Japanese philosophy that focuses on continuous improvement throughout all aspects of life. When applied to the workplace, _________ activities continually improve all functions of a business, from manufacturing to management and from the CEO to the assembly line workers. By improving standardized activities and processes, _________ aims to eliminate waste .

a. Cross-docking
b. Sensitivity analysis
c. Kaizen
d. Psychological pricing

35. In decision theory and estimation theory, the _________ of an estimator, $\hat{\theta}$, of an unknown parameter of the distribution, θ, is the expected value of the loss function

$$R(\theta,\hat{\theta}) = \mathbb{E}_\theta L(\theta,\hat{\theta}) = \int L(\theta,\hat{\theta})\, dP_\theta.$$

where dP_θ is a probability measure parametrized by θ.

- For a scalar parameter θ and a quadratic loss function,

$$L(\theta,\hat{\theta}) = (\theta - \hat{\theta})^2$$

the _________ function becomes the mean squared error of the estimate,

$$R(\theta,\hat{\theta}) = E_\theta(\theta - \hat{\theta})^2$$

- In density estimation, the unknown parameter is probability density itself. The loss function is typically chosen to be a norm in an appropriate function space. For example, for L^2 norm,

$$L(f,\hat{f}) = \|f - \hat{f}\|_2^2$$

the _________ function becomes the mean integrated squared error

$$R(f,\hat{f}) = E\|f - \hat{f}\|^2$$

.

a. Risk aversion
b. Risk
c. Linear model
d. Financial modeling

36. _________ is a type of trade policy that allows traders to act and transact without interference from government. Thus, the policy permits trading partners mutual gains from trade, with goods and services produced according to the theory of comparative advantage.

Under a _________ policy, prices are a reflection of true supply and demand, and are the sole determinant of resource allocation.

a. 1990 Clean Air Act
b. 28-hour day
c. 33 Strategies of War
d. Free trade

37. In economics and sociology, an _________ is any factor (financial or non-financial) that enables or motivates a particular course of action, or counts as a reason for preferring one choice to the alternatives. It is an expectation that encourages people to behave in a certain way. Since human beings are purposeful creatures, the study of _________ structures is central to the study of all economic activity (both in terms of individual decision-making and in terms of co-operation and competition within a larger institutional structure.)

a. AAAI
b. A4e
c. Incentive
d. A Stake in the Outcome

38. The _________ is a trilateral trade bloc in North America created by the governments of the United States, Canada, and Mexico. The agreement creating the trade bloc came into force on January 1, 1994. It superseded the Canada-United States Free Trade Agreement between the U.S. and Canada.

a. Trade union
b. Business war game
c. Career portfolios
d. North American Free Trade Agreement

39. The _________ captures an expanded spectrum of values and criteria for measuring organizational success: economic, ecological and social. With the ratification of the United Nations and ICLEI _________ standard for urban and community accounting in early 2007, this became the dominant approach to public sector full cost accounting. Similar UN standards apply to natural capital and human capital measurement to assist in measurements required by _________, e.g. the ecoBudget standard for reporting ecological footprint.

a. 28-hour day
b. 33 Strategies of War
c. Triple bottom line
d. 1990 Clean Air Act

40. A _________ is a compensation, usually financial, received by a worker in exchange for their labor.

Compensation in terms of _________s is given to worker and compensation in terms of salary is given to employees. Compensation is a monetary benefits given to employees in returns of the services provided by them.

a. Wage
b. Performance-related pay
c. Profit-sharing agreement
d. State Compensation Insurance Fund

41. In business and engineering, new _________ is the term used to describe the complete process of bringing a new product or service to market. There are two parallel paths involved in the NProduct development process: one involves the idea generation, product design, and detail engineering; the other involves market research and marketing analysis. Companies typically see new _________ as the first stage in generating and commercializing new products within the overall strategic process of product life cycle management used to maintain or grow their market share.

a. 1990 Clean Air Act
b. Product development
c. 33 Strategies of War
d. 28-hour day

42. _________ is an area of business concerned with the production of goods and services, and involves the responsibility of ensuring that business operations are efficient in terms of using as little resource as needed, and effective in terms of meeting customer requirements. It is concerned with managing the process that converts inputs (in the forms of materials, labour and energy) into outputs (in the form of goods and services.)

Operations traditionally refers to the production of goods and services separately, although the distinction between these two main types of operations is increasingly difficult to make as manufacturers tend to merge product and service offerings.

a. AAAI
b. A4e
c. A Stake in the Outcome
d. Operations management

43. An _________ is a situation that will often involve an apparent conflict between moral imperatives, in which to obey one would result in transgressing another. This is also called an ethical paradox since in moral philosophy, paradox plays a central role in ethics debates. For instance, an ethical admonition to 'love thy neighbour as thy self' is not always just in contrast with, but sometimes in contradiction to an armed neighbour actively trying to kill you: if he or she succeeds, you will not be able to love him or her.

a. A Stake in the Outcome
b. A4e
c. AAAI
d. Ethical dilemma

44. _________ is a type of thought exhibited by group members who try to minimize conflict and reach consensus without critically testing, analyzing, and evaluating ideas. Individual creativity, uniqueness, and independent thinking are lost in the pursuit of group cohesiveness, as are the advantages of reasonable balance in choice and thought that might normally be obtained by making decisions as a group. During _________, members of the group avoid promoting viewpoints outside the comfort zone of consensus thinking.

a. Diffusion of responsibility
b. Groupthink
c. Psychological statistics
d. Self-report inventory

1. _________ is a sub-topic of machine learning. It is 'the act of taking in raw data and taking an action based on the category of the data'. Most research in _________ is about methods for supervised learning and unsupervised learning.

a. 28-hour day
b. 1990 Clean Air Act
c. 33 Strategies of War
d. Pattern recognition

2. _________ is a process of planning and controlling the performance or execution of any type of activity, such as:

- a project (project _________) or
- a process (process _________, sometimes referred to as the process performance measurement and management system.)

Organization's senior management is responsible for carrying out its _________.

a. Participatory management
b. Management process
c. Work design
d. Human Relations Movement

3. A _________ is a type of business entity in which partners (owners) share with each other the profits or losses of the business. _________s are often favored over corporations for taxation purposes, as the _________ structure does not generally incur a tax on profits before it is distributed to the partners (i.e. there is no dividend tax levied.) However, depending on the _________ structure and the jurisdiction in which it operates, owners of a _________ may be exposed to greater personal liability than they would as shareholders of a corporation.

a. Mediation
b. Due process
c. Federal Employers Liability Act
d. Partnership

4. _________ is a method by which the job performance of an employee is evaluated _________ is a part of career development.

_________s are regular reviews of employee performance within organizations

Generally, the aims of a _________ are to:

- Give feedback on performance to employees.
- Identify employee training needs.
- Document criteria used to allocate organizational rewards.
- Form a basis for personnel decisions: salary increases, promotions, disciplinary actions, etc.
- Provide the opportunity for organizational diagnosis and development.
- Facilitate communication between employee and administraton
- Validate selection techniques and human resource policies to meet federal Equal Employment Opportunity requirements.

A common approach to assessing performance is to use a numerical or scalar rating system whereby managers are asked to score an individual against a number of objectives/attributes. In some companies, employees receive assessments from their manager, peers, subordinates and customers while also performing a self assessment.

a. Personnel management
b. Human resource management
c. Progressive discipline
d. Performance appraisal

5. _________ refers to a range of skills, tools, and techniques used to manage time when accomplishing specific tasks, projects and goals. This set encompass a wide scope of activities, and these include planning, allocating, setting goals, delegation, analysis of time spent, monitoring, organizing, scheduling, and prioritizing. Initially _________ referred to just business or work activities, but eventually the term broadened to include personal activities also.

a. Voice of the customer
b. Cash cow
c. Formula for Change
d. Time management

6. A _________ is a brief written statement of the purpose of a company or organization. Ideally, a _________ guides the actions of the organization, spells out its overall goal, provides a sense of direction, and guides decision making for all levels of management.

_________s often contain the following:

- Purpose and aim of the organization
- The organization's primary stakeholders: clients, stockholders, etc.
- Responsibilities of the organization toward these stakeholders
- Products and services offered

In developing a _________:

- Encourage as much input as feasible from employees, volunteers, and other stakeholders
- Publicize it broadly

The _________ can be used to resolve differences between business stakeholders. Stakeholders include: employees including managers and executives, stockholders, board of directors, customers, suppliers, distributors, creditors, governments (local, state, federal, etc.), unions, competitors, NGO's, and the general public.

a. 33 Strategies of War
b. 28-hour day
c. 1990 Clean Air Act
d. Mission statement

7. An _________ is a subset of strategic work plan. It describes short-term ways of achieving milestones and explains how, or what portion of, a strategic plan will be put into operation during a given operational period, in the case of commercial application, a fiscal year or another given budgetary term. An operational plan is the basis for, and justification of an annual operating budget request.

a. A Stake in the Outcome
b. AAAI
c. Operational planning
d. A4e

8. The _________ captures an expanded spectrum of values and criteria for measuring organizational success: economic, ecological and social. With the ratification of the United Nations and ICLEI _________ standard for urban and community accounting in early 2007, this became the dominant approach to public sector full cost accounting. Similar UN standards apply to natural capital and human capital measurement to assist in measurements required by _________, e.g. the ecoBudget standard for reporting ecological footprint.

a. 33 Strategies of War
b. Triple bottom line
c. 1990 Clean Air Act
d. 28-hour day

9. _________ is an organization's process of defining its strategy and making decisions on allocating its resources to pursue this strategy, including its capital and people. Various business analysis techniques can be used in _________, including SWOT analysis (Strengths, Weaknesses, Opportunities, and Threats) and PEST analysis (Political, Economic, Social, and Technological analysis) or STEER analysis involving Socio-cultural, Technological, Economic, Ecological, and Regulatory factors and EPISTEL (Environment, Political, Informatic, Social, Technological, Economic and Legal)

_________ is the formal consideration of an organization's future course. All _________ deals with at least one of three key questions:

1. 'What do we do?'
2. 'For whom do we do it?'
3. 'How do we excel?'

In business _________, the third question is better phrased 'How can we beat or avoid competition?'. (Bradford and Duncan, page 1.)

a. 33 Strategies of War
b. Strategic planning
c. 28-hour day
d. 1990 Clean Air Act

10. _________ involves establishing specific, measurable and time-targeted objectives. Work on the theory of goal-setting suggests that it's an effective tool for making progress by ensuring that participants in a group with a common goal are clearly aware of what is expected from them if an objective is to be achieved. On a personal level, setting goals is a process that allows people to specify then work towards their own objectives - most commonly with financial or career-based goals.

a. Catfish effect
b. Resource-based view
c. Digital strategy
d. Goal setting

11. _________ is one of the managerial functions like planning, organizing, staffing and directing. It is an important function because it helps to check the errors and to take the corrective action so that deviation from standards are minimized and stated goals of the organization are achieved in desired manner.According to modern concepts, _________ is a foreseeing action whereas earlier concept of _________ was used only when errors were detected. _________ in management means setting standards, measuring actual performance and taking corrective action.

a. Turnover
b. Decision tree pruning
c. Schedule of reinforcement
d. Control

12. _________ comprises a range of practices used in an organisation to identify, create, represent, distribute and enable adoption of insights and experiences. Such insights and experiences comprise knowledge, either embodied in individuals or embedded in organisational processes or practice.

An established discipline since 1991 , _________ includes courses taught in the fields of business administration, information systems, management, and library and information sciences .

a. 1990 Clean Air Act
b. 28-hour day
c. 33 Strategies of War
d. Knowledge management

13. _________ is a process of agreeing upon objectives within an organization so that management and employees agree to the objectives and understand what they are in the organization.

The term '_________' was first popularized by Peter Drucker in his 1954 book 'The Practice of Management'.

The essence of _________ is participative goal setting, choosing course of actions and decision making.

a. Job enrichment
b. Business economics
c. Clean sheet review
d. Management by Objectives

14. _________ refers to the movement of cash into or out of a business or financial product. It is usually measured during a specified, finite period of time. Measurement of _________ can be used

- to determine a project's rate of return or value. The time of _________s into and out of projects are used as inputs in financial models such as internal rate of return, and net present value.
- to determine problems with a business's liquidity. Being profitable does not necessarily mean being liquid. A company can fail because of a shortage of cash, even while profitable.
- as an alternate measure of a business's profits when it is believed that accrual accounting concepts do not represent economic realities. For example, a company may be notionally profitable but generating little operational cash (as may be the case for a company that barters its products rather than selling for cash.) In such a case, the company may be deriving additional operating cash by issuing shares evaluating default risk, re-investment requirements, etc.

_________ is a generic term used differently depending on the context. It may be defined by users for their own purposes.

a. Gross profit margin
b. Gross profit
c. Sweat equity
d. Cash flow

15. _________ is the discipline of planning, organizing and managing resources to bring about the successful completion of specific project goals and objectives. It is often closely related to and sometimes conflated with Program management.

A project is a finite endeavor--having specific start and completion dates--undertaken to meet particular goals and objectives, usually to bring about beneficial change or added value.

a. Precedence diagram
b. Project management
c. Project engineer
d. Work package

16. A _________ is a compensation, usually financial, received by a worker in exchange for their labor.

Compensation in terms of _________s is given to worker and compensation in terms of salary is given to employees. Compensation is a monetary benefits given to employees in returns of the services provided by them.

a. State Compensation Insurance Fund
b. Performance-related pay
c. Profit-sharing agreement
d. Wage

17. A _________ in today's workforce is an individual that is valued for their ability to interpret information within a specific subject area. They will often advance the overall understanding of that subject through focused analysis, design and/or development. They use research skills to define problems and to identify alternatives.

a. Customer satisfaction
b. Business rule
c. Knowledge worker
d. Career development

18. The _________ is the labour pool in employment. It is generally used to describe those working for a single company or industry, but can also apply to a geographic region like a city, country, state, etc. The term generally excludes the employers or management, and implies those involved in manual labour.

a. Workforce
b. Work-life balance
c. Pink-collar worker
d. Division of labour

19. _________ is a term defined by the Oxford English Dictionary as an individual's 'course or progress through life '. It is usually considered to pertain to remunerative work (and sometimes also formal education.)

The etymology of the term is somewhat ironic in that it comes from the Latin word carrera, which means race .

a. Career
b. Nursing shortage
c. Spatial mismatch
d. Career planning

20. _________ is a subset of career management. _________ applies the concepts of Strategic planning and Marketing to taking charge of one's professional future.

a. Career planning
b. TDY
c. Forced retention
d. Military recruitment

21. _________ has been described as the 'process of social influence in which one person can enlist the aid and support of others in the accomplishment of a common task' . A definition more inclusive of followers comes from Alan Keith of Genentech who said '_________ is ultimately about creating a way for people to contribute to making something extraordinary happen.'

_________ is one of the most salient aspects of the organizational context. However, defining _________ has been challenging.

a. 28-hour day
b. Leadership
c. Situational leadership
d. 1990 Clean Air Act

22. _________ is the strategic and coherent approach to the management of an organisation's most valued assets - the people working there who individually and collectively contribute to the achievement of the objectives of the business. The terms '_________' and 'human resources' (HR) have largely replaced the term 'personnel management' as a description of the processes involved in managing people in organizations. In simple sense, _________ means employing people, developing their resources, utilizing, maintaining and compensating their services in tune with the job and organizational requirement.

a. Progressive discipline
b. Human resource management
c. Job knowledge
d. Revolving door syndrome

23. _________ is a type of trade policy that allows traders to act and transact without interference from government. Thus, the policy permits trading partners mutual gains from trade, with goods and services produced according to the theory of comparative advantage.

Under a _________ policy, prices are a reflection of true supply and demand, and are the sole determinant of resource allocation.

a. 33 Strategies of War
b. Free trade
c. 28-hour day
d. 1990 Clean Air Act

24. A _________, in business matters, is an entity that is controlled by a bigger and more powerful entity. The controlled entity is called a company, corporation, or limited liability company and in some cases can be a government or state-owned enterprise, and the controlling entity is called its parent (or the parent company.) The reason for this distinction is that a lone company cannot be a _________ of any organization; only an entity representing a legal fiction as a separate entity can be a _________.

a. 1990 Clean Air Act
b. 28-hour day
c. 33 Strategies of War
d. Subsidiary

1. _________ is the process of comparing the cost, cycle time, productivity, or quality of a specific process or method to another that is widely considered to be an industry standard or best practice. Essentially, _________ provides a snapshot of the performance of your business and helps you understand where you are in relation to a particular standard. The result is often a business case for making changes in order to make improvements.

a. Cost leadership
b. Competitive heterogeneity
c. Complementors
d. Benchmarking

2. A _________ is a brief written statement of the purpose of a company or organization. Ideally, a _________ guides the actions of the organization, spells out its overall goal, provides a sense of direction, and guides decision making for all levels of management.

_________s often contain the following:

- Purpose and aim of the organization
- The organization's primary stakeholders: clients, stockholders, etc.
- Responsibilities of the organization toward these stakeholders
- Products and services offered

In developing a _________:

- Encourage as much input as feasible from employees, volunteers, and other stakeholders
- Publicize it broadly

The _________ can be used to resolve differences between business stakeholders. Stakeholders include: employees including managers and executives, stockholders, board of directors, customers, suppliers, distributors, creditors, governments (local, state, federal, etc.), unions, competitors, NGO's, and the general public.

a. Mission statement
b. 1990 Clean Air Act
c. 28-hour day
d. 33 Strategies of War

3. The _________ captures an expanded spectrum of values and criteria for measuring organizational success: economic, ecological and social. With the ratification of the United Nations and ICLEI _________ standard for urban and community accounting in early 2007, this became the dominant approach to public sector full cost accounting. Similar UN standards apply to natural capital and human capital measurement to assist in measurements required by _________, e.g. the ecoBudget standard for reporting ecological footprint.

a. Triple bottom line
b. 33 Strategies of War
c. 1990 Clean Air Act
d. 28-hour day

4. _________ is an organization's process of defining its strategy and making decisions on allocating its resources to pursue this strategy, including its capital and people. Various business analysis techniques can be used in _________, including SWOT analysis (Strengths, Weaknesses, Opportunities, and Threats) and PEST analysis (Political, Economic, Social, and Technological analysis) or STEER analysis involving Socio-cultural, Technological, Economic, Ecological, and Regulatory factors and EPISTEL (Environment, Political, Informatic, Social, Technological, Economic and Legal)

_________ is the formal consideration of an organization's future course. All _________ deals with at least one of three key questions:

1. 'What do we do?'
2. 'For whom do we do it?'
3. 'How do we excel?'

In business _________, the third question is better phrased 'How can we beat or avoid competition?'. (Bradford and Duncan, page 1.)

a. 28-hour day
b. 1990 Clean Air Act
c. 33 Strategies of War
d. Strategic planning

5. _________ is a term defined by the Oxford English Dictionary as an individual's 'course or progress through life '. It is usually considered to pertain to remunerative work (and sometimes also formal education.)

The etymology of the term is somewhat ironic in that it comes from the Latin word carrera, which means race .

a. Spatial mismatch
b. Nursing shortage
c. Career
d. Career planning

6. _________ is, in very basic words, a position a firm occupies against its competitors.

According to Michael Porter, the three methods for creating a sustainable _________ are through:

1. Cost leadership

2. Differentiation

3. Focus (economics)

a. 1990 Clean Air Act
b. 28-hour day
c. Theory Z
d. Competitive advantage

7. _________ can be regarded as an outcome of mental processes (cognitive process) leading to the selection of a course of action among several alternatives. Every _________ process produces a final choice. The output can be an action or an opinion of choice.

a. 28-hour day
b. 1990 Clean Air Act
c. Decision making
d. 33 Strategies of War

8. A _________ is a decision support tool that uses a tree-like graph or model of decisions and their possible consequences, including chance event outcomes, resource costs, and utility. _________s are commonly used in operations research, specifically in decision analysis, to help identify a strategy most likely to reach a goal. Another use of _________s is as a descriptive means for calculating conditional probabilities.

a. 28-hour day
b. 33 Strategies of War
c. 1990 Clean Air Act
d. Decision tree

9. _________ according to Onuoha (2007) is the practice of starting new organizations or revitalizing mature organizations, particularly new businesses generally in response to identified opportunities. _________ is often a difficult undertaking, as a vast majority of new businesses fail. Entrepreneurial activities are substantially different depending on the type of organization that is being started.

a. Entrepreneurship
b. A Stake in the Outcome
c. AAAI
d. A4e

10. _________ is a broad label that refers to any individuals or households that use goods and services generated within the economy. The concept of a _________ is used in different contexts, so that the usage and significance of the term may vary.

Typically when business people and economists talk of _________s they are talking about person as _________, an aggregated commodity item with little individuality other than that expressed in the buy/not-buy decision.

a. Consumer
b. 1990 Clean Air Act
c. 33 Strategies of War
d. 28-hour day

11. _________ Management is the succession of strategies used by management as a product goes through its _________. The conditions in which a product is sold changes over time and must be managed as it moves through its succession of stages.

The _________ goes through many phases, involves many professional disciplines, and requires many skills, tools and processes.

a. Strategic Alliance
b. Product life cycle
c. Golden handshake
d. Job hunting

12. _________ is one of the managerial functions like planning, organizing, staffing and directing. It is an important function because it helps to check the errors and to take the corrective action so that deviation from standards are minimized and stated goals of the organization are achieved in desired manner.According to modern concepts, _________ is a foreseeing action whereas earlier concept of _________ was used only when errors were detected. _________ in management means setting standards, measuring actual performance and taking corrective action.

a. Turnover
b. Control
c. Schedule of reinforcement
d. Decision tree pruning

13. _________ describes the situation when output from (or information about the result of) an event or phenomenon in the past will influence the same event/phenomenon in the present or future. When an event is part of a chain of cause-and-effect that forms a circuit or loop, then the event is said to 'feed back' into itself.

_________ is also a synonym for:

- _________ signal; the information about the initial event that is the basis for subsequent modification of the event.
- _________ loop; the causal path that leads from the initial generation of the _________ signal to the subsequent modification of the event.

_________ is a mechanism, process or signal that is looped back to control a system within itself. Such a loop is called a _________ loop.

a. Feedback
b. Feedback loop
c. 1990 Clean Air Act
d. Positive feedback

14. Feedback describes the situation when output from (or information about the result of) an event or phenomenon in the past will influence the same event/phenomenon in the present or future. When an event is part of a chain of cause-and-effect that forms a circuit or loop, then the event is said to 'feed back' into itself.

Feedback is also a synonym for:

- Feedback signal; the information about the initial event that is the basis for subsequent modification of the event.
- _________; the causal path that leads from the initial generation of the feedback signal to the subsequent modification of the event.

Feedback is a mechanism, process or signal that is looped back to control a system within itself. Such a loop is called a _________.

a. Positive feedback
b. 1990 Clean Air Act
c. Negative feedback
d. Feedback loop

15. _________ has been described as the 'process of social influence in which one person can enlist the aid and support of others in the accomplishment of a common task' . A definition more inclusive of followers comes from Alan Keith of Genentech who said '_________ is ultimately about creating a way for people to contribute to making something extraordinary happen.'

_________ is one of the most salient aspects of the organizational context. However, defining _________ has been challenging.

a. 28-hour day
b. Situational leadership
c. 1990 Clean Air Act
d. Leadership

16. _________ is a cross-disciplinary area concerned with protecting the safety, health and welfare of people engaged in work or employment. The goal of all _________ programs is to foster a work free safe environment. As a secondary effect, it may also protect co-workers, family members, employers, customers, suppliers, nearby communities, and other members of the public who are impacted by the workplace environment.

a. A4e
b. AAAI
c. A Stake in the Outcome
d. Occupational Safety and Health

17. The _________ is the primary federal law which governs occupational health and safety in the private sector and federal government in the United States. It was enacted by Congress in 1970 and was signed by President Richard Nixon on December 29, 1970. Its main goal is to ensure that employers provide employees with an environment free from recognized hazards, such as exposure to toxic chemicals, excessive noise levels, mechanical dangers, heat or cold stress, or unsanitary conditions.

a. Occupational Safety and Health Act
b. Unemployment Action Center
c. Unemployment and Farm Relief Act
d. United States Department of Justice

18. _________ is a strategic planning method used to evaluate the Strengths, Weaknesses, Opportunities, and Threats involved in a project or in a business venture. It involves specifying the objective of the business venture or project and identifying the internal and external factors that are favorable and unfavorable to achieving that objective. The technique is credited to Albert Humphrey, who led a convention at Stanford University in the 1960s and 1970s using data from Fortune 500 companies.

a. Market share
b. Corporate image
c. Marketing
d. SWOT analysis

19. _________ is a term coined by Deborah E. Meyerson used to describe corporate professionals who work toward positive change in both their work environment and the way their companies conduct business -- often taking 'radical' action that is just short of getting them fired.

In her book, _________: How Everyday Leaders Inspire Change at Work (Harvard Business School Press), Meyerson describes employees who believe and work toward creating adaptive, family-friendly, and socially responsible workplaces.

_________ are quiet leaders that act as catalysts for new ideas, alternative perspectives, and organizational learning and change -- and balance company conformity with individual rebellion.

a. 33 Strategies of War
b. 28-hour day
c. 1990 Clean Air Act
d. Tempered Radicals

20. _________ is the process of estimation in unknown situations. Prediction is a similar, but more general term. Both can refer to estimation of time series, cross-sectional or longitudinal data.

a. 1990 Clean Air Act
b. 28-hour day
c. 33 Strategies of War
d. Forecasting

21. _________ is a strategic planning method that some organizations use to make flexible long-term plans. It is in large part an adaptation and generalization of classic methods used by military intelligence.

The original method was that a group of analysts would generate simulation games for policy makers. In business applications, the emphasis on gaming the behavior of opponents was reduced (shifting more toward a game against nature). At Royal Dutch/Shell for example, _________ was viewed as changing mindsets about the exogenous part of the world, prior to formulating specific strategies.

a. Scenario planning
b. Labour productivity
c. Retroactive overtime
d. Time and attendance

22. In the social psychology of groups, _________ is the phenomenon of people making less effort to achieve a goal when they work in a group than when they work alone. This is seen as one of the main reasons groups are sometimes less productive than the combined performance of their members working as individuals.

- Ringelmann, Max : 1913

Research began in 1913 with Max Ringelmann's study. He found that when he asked a group of men to pull on a rope, that they did not pull as hard, or put as much effort into the activity, as they did when they were pulling alone.

a. Social loafing
b. Machiavellianism
c. Personal space
d. Self-enhancement

23. The term '_________' refers to the concept of collecting information and attempting to spot a pattern in the information. In some fields of study, the term '_________' has more formally-defined meanings.

In project management _________ is a mathematical technique that uses historical results to predict future outcome.

a. Least squares
b. Regression analysis
c. Stepwise regression
d. Trend analysis

24. A _________ is a process in which a potential employee is evaluated by an employer for prospective employment in their company, organization and was established in the late 16th century.

A _________ typically precedes the hiring decision, and is used to evaluate the candidate. The interview is usually preceded by the evaluation of submitted résumés from interested candidates, then selecting a small number of candidates for interviews.

a. Job interview
b. Supported employment
c. Payrolling
d. Split shift

25. _________ is an effective method of monitoring a process through the use of control charts. Control charts enable the use of objective criteria for distinguishing background variation from events of significance based on statistical techniques. Much of its power lies in the ability to monitor both process center and its variation about that center.

a. Single Minute Exchange of Die
b. Statistical process control
c. Process capability
d. Quality control

26. Social consciousness is consciousness shared within a society. It can also be defined as _________; to be aware of the problems that different societies and communities face on a day-to-day basis; to be conscious of the difficulties and hardships of society.

There is debate as to exactly what the term means.

a. Role conflict
b. Self-disclosure
c. Soft skill
d. Social awareness

27. A broad definition of _________ is the action of gathering, analyzing, and distributing information about products, customers, competitors and any aspect of the environment needed to support executives and managers in making strategic decisions for an organization.

Key points of this definitions:

1. _________ is an ethical and legal business practice. (This is important as _________ professionals emphasize that the discipline is not the same as industrial espionage which is both unethical and usually illegal.)
2. The focus is on the external business environment.
3. There is a process involved in gathering information, converting it into intelligence and then utilizing this in business decision making. _________ professionals emphasize that if the intelligence gathered is not usable (or actionable) then it is not intelligence.

A more focused definition of _________ regards it as the organizational function responsible for the early identification of risks and opportunities in the market before they become obvious. Experts also call this process the early signal analysis. This definition focuses attention on the difference between dissemination of widely available factual information (such as market statistics, financial reports, newspaper clippings) performed by functions such as libraries and information centers, and _________ which is a perspective on developments and events aimed at yielding a competitive edge.

a. Competitive intelligence
b. 1990 Clean Air Act
c. 28-hour day
d. Competitor or Competitive Intelligence

28. _________ refers to various methodologies for analyzing the requirements of a job.

The general purpose of _________ is to document the requirements of a job and the work performed. Job and task analysis is performed as a basis for later improvements, including: definition of a job domain; describing a job; developing performance appraisals, selection systems, promotion criteria, training needs assessment, and compensation plans.

a. Hersey-Blanchard situational theory
b. Work design
c. Management process
d. Job analysis

29. _________ is the term used to describe a situation where different entities cooperate advantageously for a final outcome. Simply defined, it means that the whole is greater than the sum of the individual parts. Although the whole will be greater than each individual part, this is not the concept of _________.

a. 28-hour day
b. 1990 Clean Air Act
c. 33 Strategies of War
d. Synergy

30. The _________ is a performance management tool for measuring whether the smaller-scale operational activities of a company are aligned with its larger-scale objectives in terms of vision and strategy.

By focusing not only on financial outcomes but also on the operational, marketing and developmental inputs to these, the _________ helps provide a more comprehensive view of a business, which in turn helps organizations act in their best long-term interests. This tool is also being used to address business response to climate change and greenhouse gas emissions.

a. Middle management
b. Management development
c. Commercial management
d. Balanced scorecard

31. _________ consists of the mental process of thinking involved with the process of judging the merits of multiple options and selecting one of them for action. Some simple examples include deciding whether to get up in the morning or go back to sleep, or selecting a given route for a journey. More complex examples (often decisions that affect what a person thinks or their core beliefs) include choosing a lifestyle, religious affiliation, or political position.

a. Trade study
b. Choice
c. Groups decision making
d. Championship mobilization

32. _________ is the provision of service to customers before, during and after a purchase.

According to Turban et al. (2002), '_________ is a series of activities designed to enhance the level of customer satisfaction - that is, the feeling that a product or service has met the customer expectation.'

Its importance varies by product, industry and customer; defective or broken merchandise can be exchanged, often only with a receipt and within a specified time frame.

a. 28-hour day
b. 1990 Clean Air Act
c. Service rate
d. Customer service

33. _________ is an advertisement in which a particular product specifically mentions a competitor by name for the express purpose of showing why the competitor is inferior to the product naming it.

This should not be confused with parody advertisements, where a fictional product is being advertised for the purpose of poking fun at the particular advertisement, nor should it be confused with the use of a coined brand name for the purpose of comparing the product without actually naming an actual competitor. ('Wikipedia tastes better and is less filling than the Encyclopedia Galactica.')

In the 1980s, during what has been referred to as the cola wars, soft-drink manufacturer Pepsi ran a series of advertisements where people, caught on hidden camera, in a blind taste test, chose Pepsi over rival Coca-Cola.

a. 1990 Clean Air Act
b. 33 Strategies of War
c. 28-hour day
d. Comparative advertising

34. An _________ is a tax levied on the financial income of people, corporations, or other legal entities. Various _________ systems exist, with varying degrees of tax incidence. Income taxation can be progressive, proportional, or regressive.

a. Ordinary income
b. A Stake in the Outcome
c. A4e
d. Income tax

35. An _________ is a situation that will often involve an apparent conflict between moral imperatives, in which to obey one would result in transgressing another. This is also called an ethical paradox since in moral philosophy, paradox plays a central role in ethics debates. For instance, an ethical admonition to 'love thy neighbour as thy self' is not always just in contrast with, but sometimes in contradiction to an armed neighbour actively trying to kill you: if he or she succeeds, you will not be able to love him or her.

a. A4e
b. AAAI
c. A Stake in the Outcome
d. Ethical dilemma

1. _________ can be regarded as an outcome of mental processes (cognitive process) leading to the selection of a course of action among several alternatives. Every _________ process produces a final choice. The output can be an action or an opinion of choice.

a. 1990 Clean Air Act
b. 28-hour day
c. 33 Strategies of War
d. Decision making

2. The 'business case for _________', theorizes that in a global marketplace, a company that employs a diverse workforce (both men and women, people of many generations, people from ethnically and racially diverse backgrounds etc.) is better able to understand the demographics of the marketplace it serves and is thus better equipped to thrive in that marketplace than a company that has a more limited range of employee demographics.

An additional corollary suggests that a company that supports the _________ of its workforce can also improve employee satisfaction, productivity and retention.

a. Virtual team
b. Trademark
c. Diversity
d. Kanban

3. _________ is the state or fact of exclusive rights and control over property, which may be an object, land/real estate or intellectual property. An _________ right is also referred to as title. The concept of _________ has existed for thousands of years and in all cultures.

a. A4e
b. A Stake in the Outcome
c. Emanation of the state
d. Ownership

4. Organizational culture is not the same as _________. It is wider and deeper concepts, something that an organization 'is' rather than what it 'has' (according to Buchanan and Huczynski.)

_________ is the total sum of the values, customs, traditions and meanings that make a company unique.

a. Work design
b. Job analysis
c. Path-goal theory
d. Corporate culture

5. Engineering _________ is the permissible limit of variation in

1. a physical dimension,
2. a measured value or physical property of a material, manufactured object, system, or service,
3. other measured values (such as temperature, humidity, etc.)
4. in engineering and safety, a physical distance or space (_________), as in a truck (lorry), train or boat under a bridge as well as a train in a tunnel

Dimensions, properties, or conditions may vary within certain practical limits without significantly affecting functioning of equipment or a process. _________s are specified to allow reasonable leeway for imperfections and inherent variability without compromising performance.

The _________ may be specified as a factor or percentage of the nominal value, a maximum deviation from a nominal value, an explicit range of allowed values, be specified by a note or published standard with this information, or be implied by the numeric accuracy of the nominal value. _________ can be symmetrical, as in 40±0.1, or asymmetrical, such as 40+0.2/−0.1.

a. Quality assurance
b. Root cause analysis
c. Zero defects
d. Tolerance

6. _________ is a contract between two parties, one being the employer and the other being the employee. An employee may be defined as: 'A person in the service of another under any contract of hire, express or implied, oral or written, where the employer has the power or right to control and direct the employee in the material details of how the work is to be performed.' Black's Law Dictionary page 471 (5th ed. 1979.)

a. Employment
b. Employment rate
c. Exit interview
d. Employment counsellor

7. The process of _________ involves the introduction of a good or service that is new or substantially improved. This includes, but is not limited to, improvements in functional characteristics, technical abilities, or ease of use.

a. Service-profit chain
b. Job enlargement
c. Letter of resignation
d. Product innovation

8. The _________ (Pub.L. 93-406, 88 Stat. 829, enacted September 2, 1974) is an American federal statute that establishes minimum standards for pension plans in private industry and provides for extensive rules on the federal income tax effects of transactions associated with employee benefit plans.

a. A Stake in the Outcome
b. AAAI
c. A4e
d. Employee Retirement Income Security Act of 1974

9. _________ is the point where a person stops employment completely. A person may also semi-retire and keep some sort of _________ job, out of choice rather than necessity. This usually happens upon reaching a determined age, when physical conditions don't allow the person to work any more (by illness or accident), or even for personal choice (usually in the presence of an adequate pension or personal savings.)

a. Termination of employment
b. Severance package
c. Wrongful dismissal
d. Retirement

10. The '_________' states that any purposeful action will produce some unintended consequences. A classic example is a bypass -- a road built to relieve traffic congestion on a congested road -- that attracts new development and with it more traffic, resulting in two congested streets instead of one.

This maxim is not a scientific law; it is more in line with Murphy's law as a warning against the hubristic belief that humans can fully control the world around them.

a. 33 Strategies of War
b. 1990 Clean Air Act
c. 28-hour day
d. Law of Unintended Consequences

11. _________ are outcomes that are not (or not limited to) the results originally intended in a particular situation. The unintended results may be foreseen or unforeseen, but they should be the logical or likely results of the action. For example, historians have speculated that if the Treaty of Versailles had not imposed such harsh conditions on Germany, World War II would not have occurred.

a. Unintended consequences
b. A4e
c. A Stake in the Outcome
d. AAAI

12. _________ is a concept based on the fact that rationality of individuals is limited by the information they have, the cognitive limitations of their minds, and the finite amount of time they have to make decisions. This contrasts with the concept of rationality as optimization. Another way to look at _________ is that, because decision-makers lack the ability and resources to arrive at the optimal solution, they instead apply their rationality only after having greatly simplified the choices available.

a. Mixed strategy
b. Bounded rationality
c. Complete information
d. Transferable utility

13. The phrase _________, according to the Organization for Economic Co-operation and Development, refers to 'creative work undertaken on a systematic basis in order to increase the stock of knowledge, including knowledge of man, culture and society, and the use of this stock of knowledge to devise new applications [sic]'

New product design and development is more than often a crucial factor in the survival of a company. In an industry that is fast changing, firms must continually revise their design and range of products. This is necessary due to continuous technology change and development as well as other competitors and the changing preference of customers.

a. Research and development
b. 28-hour day
c. 33 Strategies of War
d. 1990 Clean Air Act

14. _________ of the learning curve effect and the closely related experience curve effect express the relationship between equations for experience and efficiency or between efficiency gains and investment in the effort. The experience of 'learning curves' was first observed by the 19th Century German psychologist Hermann Ebbinghaus according to the difficulty of memorizing varying numbers of verbal stimuli, and subsequent learning about the complex processes of learning are discussed in the

.

The rule used for representing the learning curve effect states that the more times a task has been performed, the less time will be required on each subsequent iteration.

a. Spatial Decision Support Systems
b. Point biserial correlation coefficient
c. Distribution
d. Models

15. _________ comprises a range of practices used in an organisation to identify, create, represent, distribute and enable adoption of insights and experiences. Such insights and experiences comprise knowledge, either embodied in individuals or embedded in organisational processes or practice.

An established discipline since 1991 , _________ includes courses taught in the fields of business administration, information systems, management, and library and information sciences .

a. 28-hour day
b. Knowledge management
c. 33 Strategies of War
d. 1990 Clean Air Act

16. A _________ is a decision support tool that uses a tree-like graph or model of decisions and their possible consequences, including chance event outcomes, resource costs, and utility. _________s are commonly used in operations research, specifically in decision analysis, to help identify a strategy most likely to reach a goal. Another use of _________s is as a descriptive means for calculating conditional probabilities.

a. 33 Strategies of War	b. 28-hour day
c. Decision tree	d. 1990 Clean Air Act

17. The _________ is given by the United States National Institute of Standards and Technology. Through the actions of the National Productivity Advisory Committee chaired by Jack Grayson, it was established by the Malcolm Baldrige National Quality Improvement Act of 1987 - Public Law 100-107 and named for Malcolm Baldrige, who served as United States Secretary of Commerce during the Reagan administration from 1981 until his 1987 death in a rodeo accident. APQC, , organized the first White House Conference on Productivity, spearheading the creation and design of the _________ in 1987, and jointly administering the award for its first three years.

a. Scenario planning	b. Time and attendance
c. Malcolm Baldrige National Quality Award	d. Business Network Transformation

18. A _________ is a person who alleges misconduct. More complex definitions may be used, but the issue is that the _________ usually faces reprisal. The misconduct may be classified in many ways; for example, a violation of a law, rule, regulation and/or a direct threat to public interest, such as fraud, health/safety violations, and corruption.

a. Whistleblower	b. 33 Strategies of War
c. 1990 Clean Air Act	d. 28-hour day

19. The _________ was the outcome of the failure of negotiating governments to create the International Trade Organization (ITO.) GATT was formed in 1947 and lasted until 1994, when it was replaced by the World Trade Organization. The Bretton Woods Conference had introduced the idea for an organization to regulate trade as part of a larger plan for economic recovery after World War II.

a. 1990 Clean Air Act	b. Multilateral treaty
c. 28-hour day	d. General Agreement on Tariffs and Trade

20. _________ is decision making in groups consisting of multiple members/entities. The challenge of group decision is deciding what action a group should take. There are various systems designed to solve this problem.

a. Control of Substances Hazardous to Health Regulations 2002	b. Genbutsu
c. Collaborative Planning, Forecasting and Replenishment	d. Groups decision making

21. _________ is a type of thought exhibited by group members who try to minimize conflict and reach consensus without critically testing, analyzing, and evaluating ideas. Individual creativity, uniqueness, and independent thinking are lost in the pursuit of group cohesiveness, as are the advantages of reasonable balance in choice and thought that might normally be obtained by making decisions as a group. During _________, members of the group avoid promoting viewpoints outside the comfort zone of consensus thinking.

a. Self-report inventory	b. Diffusion of responsibility
c. Psychological statistics	d. Groupthink

22. _________, commonly abbreviated to Gen X, is a term used to refer to a generational cohort of children born after the baby boom ended and usually prior to the 1980s

The term _________ has been used in demography, the social sciences, and marketing, though it is most often used in popular culture.

In the U.S. _________ was originally referred to as the 'baby bust' generation because of the drop in the birth rate following the baby boom.

a. Abraham Harold Maslow
b. Adam Smith
c. Affiliation
d. Generation X

23. _________ is a term used to describe the demographic cohort following Generation X. Its members are often referred to as 'Millennials' or 'Echo Boomers') . There are no precise dates for when Gen Y begins and ends. Most commentators use dates from the early 1980s to early 1990s.

a. David Wittig
b. Generation Y
c. Giovanni Agnelli
d. Benjamin R. Barber

24. _________ is the strategic and coherent approach to the management of an organisation's most valued assets - the people working there who individually and collectively contribute to the achievement of the objectives of the business. The terms '_________' and 'human resources' (HR) have largely replaced the term 'personnel management' as a description of the processes involved in managing people in organizations. In simple sense, _________ means employing people, developing their resources, utilizing, maintaining and compensating their services in tune with the job and organizational requirement.

a. Progressive discipline
b. Revolving door syndrome
c. Job knowledge
d. Human resource management

25. _________ is an adjective for experience-based techniques that help in problem solving, learning and discovery. A _________ method is particularly used to rapidly come to a solution that is hoped to be close to the best possible answer, or 'optimal solution'. _________s are 'rules of thumb', educated guesses, intuitive judgments or simply common sense.

a. 28-hour day
b. Representativeness
c. Heuristic
d. 1990 Clean Air Act

26. _________ was first described by Barry M. Staw in his 1976 paper, 'Knee deep in the big muddy: A study of escalating commitment to a chosen course of action'. More recently the term Sunk cost fallacy has been used to describe the phenomenon where people justify increased investment in a decision, based on the cumulative prior investment, despite new evidence suggesting that the decision was probably wrong. Such investment may include money , time, or -- in the case of military strategy -- human lives.

a. Open Options
b. A4e
c. A Stake in the Outcome
d. Escalation of commitment

27. The _________ heuristic is a heuristic wherein people assume commonality between objects of similar appearance, or between an object and a group it appears to fit into. While often very useful in everyday life, it can also result in neglect of relevant base rates and other cognitive biases. The representative heuristic was first proposed by Amos Tversky and Daniel Kahneman.

a. 28-hour day
b. 1990 Clean Air Act
c. Representativeness heuristic
d. Representativeness

28. _________ is a theory that describes decisions between alternatives that involve risk, i.e. alternatives with uncertain outcomes, where the probabilities are known. The model is descriptive: it tries to model real-life choices, rather than optimal decisions.

_________ was developed by Daniel Kahneman, professor at Princeton University's Department of Psychology, and Amos Tversky in 1979 as a psychologically realistic alternative to expected utility theory.

a. 1990 Clean Air Act
b. Loss aversion
c. Prospect theory
d. Mental accounting

29. _________ Movement refers to those researchers of organizational development who study the behavior of people in groups, in particular workplace groups. It originated in the 1920s' Hawthorne studies, which examined the effects of social relations, motivation and employee satisfaction on factory productivity. The movement viewed workers in terms of their psychology and fit with companies, rather than as interchangeable parts.

a. Human relations
b. Participatory management
c. Work design
d. Hersey-Blanchard situational theory

30. The _________ captures an expanded spectrum of values and criteria for measuring organizational success: economic, ecological and social. With the ratification of the United Nations and ICLEI _________ standard for urban and community accounting in early 2007, this became the dominant approach to public sector full cost accounting. Similar UN standards apply to natural capital and human capital measurement to assist in measurements required by _________, e.g. the ecoBudget standard for reporting ecological footprint.

a. 33 Strategies of War
b. Triple bottom line
c. 1990 Clean Air Act
d. 28-hour day

31. A _________ is typically described as a deliberate plan of action to guide decisions and achieve rational outcome(s.) However, the term may also be used to denote what is actually done, even though it is unplanned.

The term may apply to government, private sector organizations and groups, and individuals.

a. 1990 Clean Air Act
b. 28-hour day
c. 33 Strategies of War
d. Policy

1. There are two types of _________ relationships: formal and informal. Informal relationships develop on their own between partners. Formal _________, on the other hand, refers to assigned relationships, often associated with organizational _________ programs designed to promote employee development or to assist at-risk children and youth.

a. Mentoring
b. Fix it twice
c. Human resource management system
d. Real Property Administrator

2. _________ is an idea in the field of Organizational studies and management which describes the psychology, attitudes, experiences, beliefs and Values (personal and cultural values) of an organization. It has been defined as 'the specific collection of values and norms that are shared by people and groups in an organization and that control the way they interact with each other and with stakeholders outside the organization.'

This definition continues to explain organizational values also known as 'beliefs and ideas about what kinds of goals members of an organization should pursue and ideas about the appropriate kinds or standards of behavior organizational members should use to achieve these goals. From organizational values develop organizational norms, guidelines or expectations that prescribe appropriate kinds of behavior by employees in particular situations and control the behavior of organizational members towards one another.'

_________ is not the same as corporate culture.

a. Organizational effectiveness
b. Union shop
c. Organizational development
d. Organizational culture

3. A _________ is a list of the general tasks and responsibilities of a position. Typically, it also includes to whom the position reports, specifications such as the qualifications needed by the person in the job, salary range for the position, etc. A _________ is usually developed by conducting a job analysis, which includes examining the tasks and sequences of tasks necessary to perform the job.

a. Recruitment Process Insourcing
b. Recruitment advertising
c. Recruitment
d. Job description

4. Human resource management (HRM) is the strategic and coherent approach to the management of an organisation's most valued assets - the people working there who individually and collectively contribute to the achievement of the objectives of the business. The terms 'human resource management' and 'human resources' (HR) have largely replaced the term '_________' as a description of the processes involved in managing people in organizations. In simple sense, HRM means employing people, developing their resources, utilizing, maintaining and compensating their services in tune with the job and organizational requirement.

a. Personnel management
b. Human resources
c. Salary
d. Progressive discipline

5. _________ is a business magazine published by McGraw-Hill. It was first published in 1929 (as The Business Week) under the direction of Malcolm Muir, who was serving as president of the McGraw-Hill Publishing company at the time. Its primary competitors in the national business magazine category are Fortune and Forbes, which are published bi-weekly.

a. The Wealth of Nations
b. Hotel Vikas
c. BusinessWeek
d. Democracy in America

6. _________ refers to the movement of cash into or out of a business or financial product. It is usually measured during a specified, finite period of time. Measurement of _________ can be used

- to determine a project's rate of return or value. The time of _________s into and out of projects are used as inputs in financial models such as internal rate of return, and net present value.
- to determine problems with a business's liquidity. Being profitable does not necessarily mean being liquid. A company can fail because of a shortage of cash, even while profitable.
- as an alternate measure of a business's profits when it is believed that accrual accounting concepts do not represent economic realities. For example, a company may be notionally profitable but generating little operational cash (as may be the case for a company that barters its products rather than selling for cash.) In such a case, the company may be deriving additional operating cash by issuing shares evaluating default risk, re-investment requirements, etc.

_________ is a generic term used differently depending on the context. It may be defined by users for their own purposes.

a. Gross profit margin
b. Gross profit
c. Sweat equity
d. Cash flow

7. _________ according to Onuoha (2007) is the practice of starting new organizations or revitalizing mature organizations, particularly new businesses generally in response to identified opportunities. _________ is often a difficult undertaking, as a vast majority of new businesses fail. Entrepreneurial activities are substantially different depending on the type of organization that is being started.

a. Entrepreneurship
b. A4e
c. A Stake in the Outcome
d. AAAI

8. An _________, or organogram(me)) is a diagram that shows the structure of an organization and the relationships and relative ranks of its parts and positions/jobs. The term is also used for similar diagrams, for example ones showing the different elements of a field of knowledge or a group of languages. The French Encyclopédie had one of the first _________s of knowledge in general.

a. A4e
b. Organizational chart
c. A Stake in the Outcome
d. AAAI

9. _________ is a method by which the job performance of an employee is evaluated _________ is a part of career development.

_________s are regular reviews of employee performance within organizations

Generally, the aims of a _________ are to:

- Give feedback on performance to employees.
- Identify employee training needs.
- Document criteria used to allocate organizational rewards.
- Form a basis for personnel decisions: salary increases, promotions, disciplinary actions, etc.
- Provide the opportunity for organizational diagnosis and development.
- Facilitate communication between employee and administraton
- Validate selection techniques and human resource policies to meet federal Equal Employment Opportunity requirements.

A common approach to assessing performance is to use a numerical or scalar rating system whereby managers are asked to score an individual against a number of objectives/attributes. In some companies, employees receive assessments from their manager, peers, subordinates and customers while also performing a self assessment.

a. Progressive discipline
b. Performance appraisal
c. Personnel management
d. Human resource management

10. In a military context, the _________ is the line of authority and responsibility along which orders are passed within a military unit and between different units. The term is also used in a civilian management context describing comparable hierarchical structures of authority.

a. French leave
b. 28-hour day
c. Chain of command
d. 1990 Clean Air Act

11. _________(known as horizontal organization) refers to an organizational structure with few or no levels of intervening management between staff and managers. The idea is that well-trained workers will be more productive when they are more directly involved in the decision making process, rather than closely supervised by many layers of management.

This structure is generally possible only in smaller organizations or individual units within larger organizations.

a. 28-hour day
b. 1990 Clean Air Act
c. 33 Strategies of War
d. Flat organization

12. _________ is a term originating in military organization theory, but now used more commonly in business management, particularly human resource management. _________ refers to the number of subordinates a supervisor has.

In the hierarchical business organization of the past it was not uncommon to see average spans of 1 to 10 or even less. That is, one manager supervised ten employees on average.

a. Span of control
b. Senior management
c. Mentoring
d. CIFMS

13. _________ is one of the managerial functions like planning, organizing, staffing and directing. It is an important function because it helps to check the errors and to take the corrective action so that deviation from standards are minimized and stated goals of the organization are achieved in desired manner.According to modern concepts, _________ is a foreseeing action whereas earlier concept of _________ was used only when errors were detected. _________ in management means setting standards, measuring actual performance and taking corrective action.

a. Decision tree pruning
b. Schedule of reinforcement
c. Control
d. Turnover

14. _________ has been described as the 'process of social influence in which one person can enlist the aid and support of others in the accomplishment of a common task' . A definition more inclusive of followers comes from Alan Keith of Genentech who said '_________ is ultimately about creating a way for people to contribute to making something extraordinary happen.'

_________ is one of the most salient aspects of the organizational context. However, defining _________ has been challenging.

a. 28-hour day
b. 1990 Clean Air Act
c. Leadership
d. Situational leadership

15. _________ is a concept in ethics with several meanings. It is often used synonymously with such concepts as responsibility, answerability, enforcement, blameworthiness, liability and other terms associated with the expectation of account-giving. As an aspect of governance, it has been central to discussions related to problems in both the public and private (corporation) worlds.

a. A Stake in the Outcome
b. A4e
c. Usury
d. Accountability

16. An _________ is a mostly hierarchical concept of subordination of entities that collaborate and contribute to serve one common aim.

Organizations are a variant of clustered entities. The structure of an organization is usually set up in many a styles, dependent on their objectives and ambience.

a. Organizational structure
b. Informal organization
c. Organizational development
d. Open shop

17. _________ is a sub-topic of machine learning. It is 'the act of taking in raw data and taking an action based on the category of the data'. Most research in _________ is about methods for supervised learning and unsupervised learning.

a. Pattern recognition
b. 1990 Clean Air Act
c. 28-hour day
d. 33 Strategies of War

18. _________ is an advertisement in which a particular product specifically mentions a competitor by name for the express purpose of showing why the competitor is inferior to the product naming it.

This should not be confused with parody advertisements, where a fictional product is being advertised for the purpose of poking fun at the particular advertisement, nor should it be confused with the use of a coined brand name for the purpose of comparing the product without actually naming an actual competitor. ('Wikipedia tastes better and is less filling than the Encyclopedia Galactica.')

In the 1980s, during what has been referred to as the cola wars, soft-drink manufacturer Pepsi ran a series of advertisements where people, caught on hidden camera, in a blind taste test, chose Pepsi over rival Coca-Cola.

a. 1990 Clean Air Act
b. Comparative advertising
c. 33 Strategies of War
d. 28-hour day

19. A _________ is a type of business entity in which partners (owners) share with each other the profits or losses of the business. _________s are often favored over corporations for taxation purposes, as the _________ structure does not generally incur a tax on profits before it is distributed to the partners (i.e. there is no dividend tax levied.) However, depending on the _________ structure and the jurisdiction in which it operates, owners of a _________ may be exposed to greater personal liability than they would as shareholders of a corporation.

a. Partnership
b. Mediation
c. Federal Employers Liability Act
d. Due process

20. _________ is a work methodology based on the parallelization of tasks (ie. concurrently.) It refers to an approach used in product development in which functions of design engineering, manufacturing engineering and other functions are integrated to reduce the elapsed time required to bring a new product to the market.

a. Concurrent engineering
b. Work package
c. Project management
d. Critical Chain Project Management

21. In business and engineering, new _________ is the term used to describe the complete process of bringing a new product or service to market. There are two parallel paths involved in the NProduct development process: one involves the idea generation, product design, and detail engineering; the other involves market research and marketing analysis. Companies typically see new _________ as the first stage in generating and commercializing new products within the overall strategic process of product life cycle management used to maintain or grow their market share.

a. 33 Strategies of War
b. 28-hour day
c. 1990 Clean Air Act
d. Product development

22. In operant conditioning, _________ occurs when an event following a response causes an increase in the probability of that response occurring in the future. Response strength can be assessed by measures such as the frequency with which the response is made (for example, a pigeon may peck a key more times in the session), or the speed with which it is made (for example, a rat may run a maze faster.) The environment change contingent upon the response is called a reinforcer.

a. Reinforcement
b. Diminishing Manufacturing Sources and Material Shortages
c. Historiometry
d. Meetings, Incentives, Conferences, and Exhibitions

23. _________ is a term defined by the Oxford English Dictionary as an individual's 'course or progress through life '. It is usually considered to pertain to remunerative work (and sometimes also formal education.)

The etymology of the term is somewhat ironic in that it comes from the Latin word carrera, which means race .

a. Career planning
b. Nursing shortage
c. Spatial mismatch
d. Career

24. In economics and sociology, an _________ is any factor (financial or non-financial) that enables or motivates a particular course of action, or counts as a reason for preferring one choice to the alternatives. It is an expectation that encourages people to behave in a certain way. Since human beings are purposeful creatures, the study of _________ structures is central to the study of all economic activity (both in terms of individual decision-making and in terms of co-operation and competition within a larger institutional structure.)

a. Incentive
b. A4e
c. AAAI
d. A Stake in the Outcome

25. A _________ or chief operations officer is a corporate officer responsible for managing the day-to-day activities of the corporation and for operations management (OM.) The _________ is one of the highest-ranking members of an organization's senior management, monitoring the daily operations of the company and reporting to the board of directors and the top executive officer, usually the chief executive officer (CEO.) The _________ is usually an executive or senior officer.

a. Chief operating officer
b. Supervisory board
c. Value based pricing
d. Product innovation

26. _________ is the life cycle of an organization from birth level to the termination.

There are five level/stages in any organization.

1. Birth
2. Growth
3. Maturity
4. Decline
5. Death

According to Richard L. Daft there are four stages in an _________.

The four stages are:

1. Entrepreneurial stage -> Crisis: Need for leadership
2. Collectivity stage -> Crisis: Need for delegation
3. Formalization stage -> Crisis: Too much red tape
4. Elaboration stage -> Crisis: Need for revitalization

(Richard L. Daft, Understanding the Theory and Design of Organizations, first edition 2007, ISBN 0-324-42271-7)

a. A Stake in the Outcome
b. Organizational life cycle
c. A4e
d. AAAI

27. A _________ or maquila is a factory that imports materials and equipment on a duty-free and tariff-free basis for assembly or manufacturing and then re-exports the assembled product, usually back to the originating country. A maquila is also referred to as a 'twin plant', or 'in-bond' industry. Nearly half a million Mexicans are employed in _________s.

a. 1990 Clean Air Act
b. Maquiladora
c. 33 Strategies of War
d. 28-hour day

28. _________ is an area of knowledge within organizational theory that studies models and theories about the way an organization learns and adapts.

In Organizational development (OD), learning is a characteristic of an adaptive organization, i.e., an organization that is able to sense changes in signals from its environment (both internal and external) and adapt accordingly.

a. AAAI
b. Organizational learning
c. A4e
d. A Stake in the Outcome

29. _________ is a recursive process where two or more people or organizations work together in an intersection of common goals -- for example, an intellectual endeavor that is creative in nature--by sharing knowledge, learning and building consensus. _________ does not require leadership and can sometimes bring better results through decentralization and egalitarianism. In particular, teams that work collaboratively can obtain greater resources, recognition and reward when facing competition for finite resources._________ is also present in opposing goals exhibiting the notion of adversarial _________, though this is not a common case for using the term.

a. 1990 Clean Air Act
b. Collectivism
c. Collaboration
d. 28-hour day

30. In decision theory and estimation theory, the _________ of an estimator, $\hat{\theta}$, of an unknown parameter of the distribution, θ, is the expected value of the loss function

$$R(\theta,\hat{\theta}) = \mathbb{E}_\theta L(\theta,\hat{\theta}) = \int L(\theta,\hat{\theta})\, dP_\theta.$$

where dP_θ is a probability measure parametrized by θ.

- For a scalar parameter θ and a quadratic loss function,

$$L(\theta,\hat{\theta}) = (\theta - \hat{\theta})^2$$

the _________ function becomes the mean squared error of the estimate,

$$R(\theta,\hat{\theta}) = E_\theta(\theta - \hat{\theta})^2$$

- In density estimation, the unknown parameter is probability density itself. The loss function is typically chosen to be a norm in an appropriate function space. For example, for L^2 norm,

$$L(f,\hat{f}) = \|f - \hat{f}\|_2^2$$

the _________ function becomes the mean integrated squared error

$$R(f,\hat{f}) = E\|f - \hat{f}\|^2$$

.

a. Linear model
b. Risk aversion
c. Financial modeling
d. Risk

31. _________ is a business management strategy, initially implemented by Motorola, that today enjoys widespread application in many sectors of industry.

_________ seeks to improve the quality of process outputs by identifying and removing the causes of defects (errors) and variation in manufacturing and business processes. It uses a set of quality management methods, including statistical methods, and creates a special infrastructure of people within the organization ('Black Belts' etc.)

a. Theory of constraints
b. Takt time
c. Production line
d. Six Sigma

32. _________ is an organization's process of defining its strategy and making decisions on allocating its resources to pursue this strategy, including its capital and people. Various business analysis techniques can be used in _________, including SWOT analysis (Strengths, Weaknesses, Opportunities, and Threats) and PEST analysis (Political, Economic, Social, and Technological analysis) or STEER analysis involving Socio-cultural, Technological, Economic, Ecological, and Regulatory factors and EPISTEL (Environment, Political, Informatic, Social, Technological, Economic and Legal)

_________ is the formal consideration of an organization's future course. All _________ deals with at least one of three key questions:

1. 'What do we do?'
2. 'For whom do we do it?'
3. 'How do we excel?'

In business _________, the third question is better phrased 'How can we beat or avoid competition?'. (Bradford and Duncan, page 1.)

a. 33 Strategies of War
b. Strategic Planning
c. 1990 Clean Air Act
d. 28-hour day

33. _________ can be regarded as an outcome of mental processes (cognitive process) leading to the selection of a course of action among several alternatives. Every _________ process produces a final choice. The output can be an action or an opinion of choice.

a. 1990 Clean Air Act
b. Decision making
c. 33 Strategies of War
d. 28-hour day

34. _________ occurs when expectant women are fired, not hired, or otherwise discriminated against due to their pregnancy or intention to become pregnant. Common forms of _________ include not being hired due to visible pregnancy or likelihood of becoming pregnant, being fired after informing an employer of one's pregnancy, being fired after maternity leave, and receiving a pay dock due to pregnancy. In the United States, since 1978, employers are legally bound to provide what insurance, leave pay, and additional support that would be bestowed upon any employee with medical leave or disability.

a. 28-hour day
b. Pregnancy Discrimination
c. 1990 Clean Air Act
d. 33 Strategies of War

35. A _________ is a compensation, usually financial, received by a worker in exchange for their labor.

Compensation in terms of _________s is given to worker and compensation in terms of salary is given to employees. Compensation is a monetary benefits given to employees in returns of the services provided by them.

a. State Compensation Insurance Fund
b. Performance-related pay
c. Profit-sharing agreement
d. Wage

36. A _________ is the term given to a company that facilitates the learning of its members and continuously transforms itself. _________s develop as a result of the pressures facing modern organizations and enables them to remain competitive in the business environment. A _________ has five main features; systems thinking, personal mastery, mental models, shared vision and team learning.

a. Quality function deployment
b. Learning organization
c. 1990 Clean Air Act
d. Hoshin Kanri

37. _________ Movement refers to those researchers of organizational development who study the behavior of people in groups, in particular workplace groups. It originated in the 1920s' Hawthorne studies, which examined the effects of social relations, motivation and employee satisfaction on factory productivity. The movement viewed workers in terms of their psychology and fit with companies, rather than as interchangeable parts.

a. Participatory management
b. Hersey-Blanchard situational theory
c. Work design
d. Human relations

38. _________ refers to those researchers of organizational development who study the behavior of people in groups, in particular workplace groups. It originated in the 1920s' Hawthorne studies, which examined the effects of social relations, motivation and employee satisfaction on factory productivity. The movement viewed workers in terms of their psychology and fit with companies, rather than as interchangeable parts.

a. Path-goal theory
b. Job analysis
c. Job satisfaction
d. Human relations movement

39. An _________ is a situation that will often involve an apparent conflict between moral imperatives, in which to obey one would result in transgressing another. This is also called an ethical paradox since in moral philosophy, paradox plays a central role in ethics debates. For instance, an ethical admonition to 'love thy neighbour as thy self' is not always just in contrast with, but sometimes in contradiction to an armed neighbour actively trying to kill you: if he or she succeeds, you will not be able to love him or her.

a. AAAI
b. A4e
c. A Stake in the Outcome
d. Ethical dilemma

1. _________ is the strategic and coherent approach to the management of an organisation's most valued assets - the people working there who individually and collectively contribute to the achievement of the objectives of the business. The terms '_________' and 'human resources' (HR) have largely replaced the term 'personnel management' as a description of the processes involved in managing people in organizations. In simple sense, _________ means employing people, developing their resources, utilizing, maintaining and compensating their services in tune with the job and organizational requirement.

a. Human resource management
b. Revolving door syndrome
c. Progressive discipline
d. Job knowledge

2. The general definition of an _________ is an evaluation of a person, organization, system, process, project or product. _________s are performed to ascertain the validity and reliability of information; also to provide an assessment of a system's internal control. The goal of an _________ is to express an opinion on the person / organization/system (etc) in question, under evaluation based on work done on a test basis.

a. A Stake in the Outcome
b. Internal control
c. Audit committee
d. Audit

3. _________ refers to the stock of skills and knowledge embodied in the ability to perform labor so as to produce economic value. It is the skills and knowledge gained by a worker through education and experience. Many early economic theories refer to it simply as labor, one of three factors of production, and consider it to be a fungible resource -- homogeneous and easily interchangeable.

a. Human capital
b. Productivity management
c. Market structure
d. Deflation

4. _________ is an increasingly broadening term with which an organization, or other human system describes the combination of traditionally administrative personnel functions with acquisition and application of skills, knowledge and experience, Employee Relations and resource planning at various levels. The field draws upon concepts developed in Industrial/Organizational Psychology and System Theory. _________ has at least two related interpretations depending on context. The original usage derives from political economy and economics, where it was traditionally called labor, one of four factors of production although this perspective is changing as a function of new and ongoing research into more strategic approaches at national levels. This first usage is used more in terms of '_________ development', and can go beyond just organizations to the level of nations . The more traditional usage within corporations and businesses refers to the individuals within a firm or agency, and to the portion of the organization that deals with hiring, firing, training, and other personnel issues, typically referred to as `_________ management'.

a. Progressive discipline
b. Bradford Factor
c. Human resource management
d. Human resources

5. _________ has been described as the 'process of social influence in which one person can enlist the aid and support of others in the accomplishment of a common task' . A definition more inclusive of followers comes from Alan Keith of Genentech who said '_________ is ultimately about creating a way for people to contribute to making something extraordinary happen.'

_________ is one of the most salient aspects of the organizational context. However, defining _________ has been challenging.

a. Situational leadership
b. 1990 Clean Air Act
c. Leadership
d. 28-hour day

6. The 'business case for _________', theorizes that in a global marketplace, a company that employs a diverse workforce (both men and women, people of many generations, people from ethnically and racially diverse backgrounds etc.) is better able to understand the demographics of the marketplace it serves and is thus better equipped to thrive in that marketplace than a company that has a more limited range of employee demographics.

An additional corollary suggests that a company that supports the _________ of its workforce can also improve employee satisfaction, productivity and retention.

a. Kanban
b. Trademark
c. Virtual team
d. Diversity

7. _________ refers to various methodologies for analyzing the requirements of a job.

The general purpose of _________ is to document the requirements of a job and the work performed. Job and task analysis is performed as a basis for later improvements, including: definition of a job domain; describing a job; developing performance appraisals, selection systems, promotion criteria, training needs assessment, and compensation plans.

a. Hersey-Blanchard situational theory
b. Work design
c. Job analysis
d. Management process

8. A _________ is a list of the general tasks and responsibilities of a position. Typically, it also includes to whom the position reports, specifications such as the qualifications needed by the person in the job, salary range for the position, etc. A _________ is usually developed by conducting a job analysis, which includes examining the tasks and sequences of tasks necessary to perform the job.

a. Recruitment advertising
b. Job description
c. Recruitment
d. Recruitment Process Insourcing

9. _________ is a mathematical science pertaining to the collection, analysis, interpretation or explanation, and presentation of data. It also provides tools for prediction and forecasting based on data. It is applicable to a wide variety of academic disciplines, from the natural and social sciences to the humanities, government and business.

a. Simple moving average
b. Location parameter
c. Failure rate
d. Statistics

10. _________ refers to techniques, processes and tools for organizing and coordinating a group of individuals working towards a common goal--i.e. a team.

Several well-known approaches to _________ have come out of academic work. Examples include the Belbin Team Inventory by Meredith Belbin, a method to identify the different types of personalities within teams, and Ken Blanchard's description of 'High Performing Teams'.

a. 1990 Clean Air Act
b. 28-hour day
c. 33 Strategies of War
d. Team management

11. In organized labor, _________ is the method whereby workers organize together (usually in unions) to meet, converse, and negotiate upon the work conditions with their employers normally resulting in a written contract setting forth the wages, hours, and other conditions to be observed for a stipulated period.It is the practice in which union and company representatives meet to negotiate a new labor contract. In various national labor and employment law contexts, the term _________ takes on a more specific legal meaning. In a broad sense, however, it is the coming together of workers to negotiate their employment.

a. Paid time off
b. Labour law
c. Labor rights
d. Collective bargaining

12. The _________ of 1938 (_________, ch. 676, 52 Stat. 1060, June 25, 1938, 29 U.S.C. ch.8), also called the Wages and Hours Bill, is United States federal law that applies to employees engaged in interstate commerce or employed by an enterprise engaged in commerce or in the production of goods for commerce, unless the employer can claim an exemption from coverage. The _________ established a national minimum wage, guaranteed time and a half for overtime in certain jobs, and prohibited most employment of minors in 'oppressive child labor,' a term defined in the statute.

a. Joint venture
b. Board of directors
c. Family and Medical Leave Act of 1993
d. Fair Labor Standards Act

13. The field of _________ looks at the relationship between management and workers, particularly groups of workers represented by a union.

_________ is an important factor in analyzing 'varieties of capitalism', such as neocorporatism, social democracy, and neoliberalism

a. Organizational effectiveness
b. Overtime
c. Informal organization
d. Industrial relations

14. _________ are conventions, treaties and recommendations designed to eliminate unjust and inhumane labour practices. The primary inernational agency charged with developing such standards is the International Labour Organization (ILO.) Established in 1919, the ILO advocates international standards as essential for the eradication of labour conditions involving 'injustice, hardship and privation'.

a. Airbus Industrie
b. Airbus SAS
c. Anaconda Copper
d. International labour standards

15. A _________ is the lowest hourly, daily or monthly wage that employers may legally pay to employees or workers. Equivalently, it is the lowest wage at which workers may sell their labor. Although _________ laws are in effect in a great many jurisdictions, there are differences of opinion about the benefits and drawbacks of a _________.

a. Deregulation
b. Rehn-Meidner Model
c. Value added
d. Minimum wage

16. _________ is the amount of time someone works beyond normal working hours. Normal hours may be determined in several ways:

- by custom (what is considered healthy or reasonable by society),
- by practices of a given trade or profession,
- by legislation,
- by agreement between employers and workers or their representatives.

Most nations have _________ laws designed to dissuade or prevent employers from forcing their employees to work excessively long hours. These laws may take into account other considerations than the humanitarian, such as increasing the overall level of employment in the economy. One common approach to regulating _________ is to require employers to pay workers at a higher hourly rate for _________ work.

a. Organizational effectiveness
b. Overtime
c. Industrial relations
d. Organizational structure

17. The _________ is a 1935 United States federal law that limits the means with which employers may react to workers in the private sector that organize labor unions, engage in collective bargaining, and take part in strikes and other forms of concerted activity in support of their demands. The Act does not, on the other hand, cover those workers who are covered by the Railway Labor Act, agricultural employees, domestic employees, supervisors, independent contractors and some close relatives of individual employers.

It was in a context of severe economic troubles that the Wagner Act came into effect.

a. 1990 Clean Air Act
b. 28-hour day
c. National Labor Relations Act
d. 33 Strategies of War

18. _________ Management is the succession of strategies used by management as a product goes through its _________. The conditions in which a product is sold changes over time and must be managed as it moves through its succession of stages.

The _________ goes through many phases, involves many professional disciplines, and requires many skills, tools and processes.

a. Job hunting
b. Strategic Alliance
c. Golden handshake
d. Product life cycle

19. A _________ is a compensation, usually financial, received by a worker in exchange for their labor.

Compensation in terms of _________s is given to worker and compensation in terms of salary is given to employees. Compensation is a monetary benefits given to employees in returns of the services provided by them.

a. State Compensation Insurance Fund
b. Profit-sharing agreement
c. Performance-related pay
d. Wage

20.

The terms _________ and positive action refer to policies that take race, ethnicity, or gender into consideration in an attempt to promote equal opportunity. The focus of such policies ranges from employment and education to public contracting and health programs. The impetus towards _________ is twofold: to maximize diversity in all levels of society, along with its presumed benefits, and to redress perceived disadvantages due to overt, institutional, or involuntary discrimination.

a. Abraham Harold Maslow
b. Affirmative action
c. Affiliation
d. Adam Smith

21. The _________ of 1990 (ADA) is the short title of United States (Pub.L. 101-336, 104 Stat. 327, enacted July 26, 1990), codified at 42 U.S.C. Â§ 12101 et seq. It was signed into law on July 26, 1990, by President George H. W. Bush, and later amended with changes effective January 1, 2009. The ADA is a wide-ranging civil rights law that prohibits, under certain circumstances, discrimination based on disability. It affords similar protections against discrimination to Americans with disabilities as the Civil Rights Act of 1964,

a. Australian labour law
b. Employment discrimination
c. Equal Pay Act of 1963
d. Americans with Disabilities Act

22. _________ is one of the managerial functions like planning, organizing, staffing and directing. It is an important function because it helps to check the errors and to take the corrective action so that deviation from standards are minimized and stated goals of the organization are achieved in desired manner.According to modern concepts, _________ is a foreseeing action whereas earlier concept of _________ was used only when errors were detected. _________ in management means setting standards, measuring actual performance and taking corrective action.

a. Schedule of reinforcement
b. Control
c. Decision tree pruning
d. Turnover

23. The _________ 1970 is an Act of the United Kingdom Parliament which prohibits any less favourable treatment between men and women in terms of pay and conditions of employment. It came into force on 29 December 1975. The term pay is interpreted in a broad sense to include, on top of wages, things like holidays, pension rights, company perks and some kinds of bonuses.

a. Australian labour law
b. Equal Pay Act
c. Oncale v. Sundowner Offshore Services
d. Architectural Barriers Act of 1968

24. The _________ is a United States labor law allowing an employee to take unpaid leave due to a serious health condition that makes the employee unable to perform his job or to care for a sick family member or to care for a new son or daughter (including by birth, adoption or foster care.) The bill was among the first signed into law by President Bill Clinton in his first term.

a. Harvester Judgment
b. Contributory negligence
c. Sarbanes-Oxley Act of 2002
d. Family and Medical Leave Act of 1993

25. _________ occurs when expectant women are fired, not hired, or otherwise discriminated against due to their pregnancy or intention to become pregnant. Common forms of _________ include not being hired due to visible pregnancy or likelihood of becoming pregnant, being fired after informing an employer of one's pregnancy, being fired after maternity leave, and receiving a pay dock due to pregnancy. In the United States, since 1978, employers are legally bound to provide what insurance, leave pay, and additional support that would be bestowed upon any employee with medical leave or disability.

a. 1990 Clean Air Act
b. 28-hour day
c. Pregnancy Discrimination
d. 33 Strategies of War

26. _________ is the point where a person stops employment completely. A person may also semi-retire and keep some sort of _________ job, out of choice rather than necessity. This usually happens upon reaching a determined age, when physical conditions don't allow the person to work any more (by illness or accident), or even for personal choice (usually in the presence of an adequate pension or personal savings.)

a. Retirement
b. Wrongful dismissal
c. Severance package
d. Termination of employment

27. The _________ of 2002 (Pub.L. 107-204, 116 Stat. 745, enacted July 30, 2002), also known as the Public Company Accounting Reform and Investor Protection Act of 2002 and commonly called Sarbanes-Oxley, Sarbox or SOX, is a United States federal law enacted on July 30, 2002, as a reaction to a number of major corporate and accounting scandals including those affecting Enron, Tyco International, Adelphia, Peregrine Systems and WorldCom.

a. Sarbanes-Oxley Act
b. Fair Labor Standards Act
c. Letter of credit
d. Sarbanes-Oxley Act of 2002

28. _________ or job seeking is the act of looking for employment, due to unemployment or discontent with a current position. The immediate goal of job seeking is usually to obtain a job interview with an employer which may lead to getting hired. The job hunter or seeker typically first looks for job vacancies or employment opportunities.

a. Psychological pricing
b. Time to market
c. First-mover advantage
d. Job hunting

29. _________ refers to the process of screening, and selecting qualified people for a job at an organization or firm mid- and large-size organizations and companies often retain professional recruiters or outsource some of the process to _________ agencies. External _________ is the process of attracting and selecting employees from outside the organization.

The _________ industry has four main types of agencies: employment agencies, _________ websites and job search engines, 'headhunters' for executive and professional _________, and in-house _________.

a. Recruitment
b. Labour hire
c. Referral recruitment
d. Recruitment Process Outsourcing

30. The _________ of 1967, Pub. L. No. 90-202, 81 Stat. 602 (Dec. 15, 1967), codified as Chapter 14 of Title 29 of the United States Code, 29 U.S.C. Â§ 621 through 29 U.S.C. Â§ 634 (ADEA), prohibits employment discrimination against persons 40 years of age or older in the United States). The law also sets standards for pensions and benefits provided by employers and requires that information about the needs of older workers be provided to the general public.

a. Undue hardship
b. Unemployment and Farm Relief Act
c. Extra time
d. Age Discrimination in Employment Act

31. _________ is a contract between two parties, one being the employer and the other being the employee. An employee may be defined as: 'A person in the service of another under any contract of hire, express or implied, oral or written, where the employer has the power or right to control and direct the employee in the material details of how the work is to be performed.' Black's Law Dictionary page 471 (5th ed. 1979.)

a. Exit interview
b. Employment counsellor
c. Employment rate
d. Employment

32. A _________ is a quantitative research method commonly employed in survey research. The aim of this approach is to ensure that each interviewee is presented with exactly the same questions in the same order. This ensures that answers can be reliably aggregated and that comparisons can be made with confidence between sample subgroups or between different survey periods.

a. Structured interview
b. Mystery shoppers
c. Questionnaire
d. Questionnaire construction

33. _________ are a method of interviews where questions can be changed or adapted to meet the respondent's intelligence, understanding or belief. Unlike a structured interview they do not offer a limited, pre-set range of answers for a respondent to choose, but instead advocate listening to how each individual person responds to the question.

The method to gather information using this technique is fairly limited, for example most surveys that are carried out via telephone or even in person tend to follow a structured method.

a. Unstructured interviews
b. A4e
c. A Stake in the Outcome
d. AAAI

34. _________ is an organization's process of defining its strategy and making decisions on allocating its resources to pursue this strategy, including its capital and people. Various business analysis techniques can be used in _________, including SWOT analysis (Strengths, Weaknesses, Opportunities, and Threats) and PEST analysis (Political, Economic, Social, and Technological analysis) or STEER analysis involving Socio-cultural, Technological, Economic, Ecological, and Regulatory factors and EPISTEL (Environment, Political, Informatic, Social, Technological, Economic and Legal)

_________ is the formal consideration of an organization's future course. All _________ deals with at least one of three key questions:

1. 'What do we do?'
2. 'For whom do we do it?'
3. 'How do we excel?'

In business _________, the third question is better phrased 'How can we beat or avoid competition?'. (Bradford and Duncan, page 1.)

a. Strategic planning
b. 1990 Clean Air Act
c. 28-hour day
d. 33 Strategies of War

35. The _________ assessment is a psychometric questionnaire designed to measure psychological preferences in how people perceive the world and make decisions.[:1] These preferences were extrapolated from the typological theories originated by Carl Gustav Jung, as published in his 1921 book Psychological Types . The original developers of the personality inventory were Katharine Cook Briggs and her daughter, Isabel Briggs Myers. They began creating the indicator during World War II, believing that a knowledge of personality preferences would help women who were entering the industrial workforce for the first time identify the sort of war-time jobs where they would be 'most comfortable and effective'.[:xiii] The initial questionnaire grew into the _________, which was first published in 1962.

a. 28-hour day
b. 1990 Clean Air Act
c. 33 Strategies of War
d. Myers-Briggs Type Indicator

36. The term _________ in logic applies to arguments or statements.

An argument is valid if and only if the truth of its premises entails the truth of its conclusion, it would be self-contradictory to affirm the premises and deny the conclusion. The corresponding conditional of a valid argument is a logical truth and the negation of its corresponding conditional is a contradiction.

a. Validity
b. 1990 Clean Air Act
c. Fuzzy logic
d. Simplification

37. _________ is a type of thought exhibited by group members who try to minimize conflict and reach consensus without critically testing, analyzing, and evaluating ideas. Individual creativity, uniqueness, and independent thinking are lost in the pursuit of group cohesiveness, as are the advantages of reasonable balance in choice and thought that might normally be obtained by making decisions as a group. During _________, members of the group avoid promoting viewpoints outside the comfort zone of consensus thinking.

a. Diffusion of responsibility
b. Self-report inventory
c. Groupthink
d. Psychological statistics

38. _________ is the provision of service to customers before, during and after a purchase.

According to Turban et al. (2002), '_________ is a series of activities designed to enhance the level of customer satisfaction - that is, the feeling that a product or service has met the customer expectation.'

Its importance varies by product, industry and customer; defective or broken merchandise can be exchanged, often only with a receipt and within a specified time frame.

a. Customer service
b. 1990 Clean Air Act
c. Service rate
d. 28-hour day

39. _________ is training for the purpose of increasing participants' cultural awareness, knowledge, and skills, which is based on the assumption that the training will benefit an organization by protecting against civil rights violations, increasing the inclusion of different identity groups, and promoting better teamwork.

_________ has been a controversial issue, due to moral considerations as well as questioned efficiency or even counterproductivity.

According to Michael Bird, many project managers may feel that they are treading new territory as they lead project teams made of individuals from different cultures, heterogeneous mixes, and differing demographics.

a. Self-disclosure
b. Diversity training
c. Role conflict
d. Soft skill

40. _________ Movement refers to those researchers of organizational development who study the behavior of people in groups, in particular workplace groups. It originated in the 1920s' Hawthorne studies, which examined the effects of social relations, motivation and employee satisfaction on factory productivity. The movement viewed workers in terms of their psychology and fit with companies, rather than as interchangeable parts.

a. Participatory management
b. Hersey-Blanchard situational theory
c. Work design
d. Human relations

41. _________ is unwelcome harassment of a sexual nature, or based upon the receiving party's sex or gender. In some contexts or circumstances, _________ may be illegal. It includes a range of behavior from seemingly mild transgressions and annoyances to actual sexual abuse or sexual assault.

a. 1990 Clean Air Act
b. Hypernorms
c. 28-hour day
d. Sexual harassment

42. _________ is an advertisement in which a particular product specifically mentions a competitor by name for the express purpose of showing why the competitor is inferior to the product naming it.

This should not be confused with parody advertisements, where a fictional product is being advertised for the purpose of poking fun at the particular advertisement, nor should it be confused with the use of a coined brand name for the purpose of comparing the product without actually naming an actual competitor. ('Wikipedia tastes better and is less filling than the Encyclopedia Galactica.')

In the 1980s, during what has been referred to as the cola wars, soft-drink manufacturer Pepsi ran a series of advertisements where people, caught on hidden camera, in a blind taste test, chose Pepsi over rival Coca-Cola.

a. 28-hour day
b. Comparative advertising
c. 1990 Clean Air Act
d. 33 Strategies of War

43. _________ is an approach to management development where an individual is moved through a schedule of assignments designed to give him or her a breadth of exposure to the entire operation.

_________ is also practiced to allow qualified employees to gain more insights into the processes of a company, and to reduce boredom and increase job satisfaction through job variation.

The term _________ can also mean the scheduled exchange of persons in offices, especially in public offices, prior to the end of incumbency or the legislative period.

a. 33 Strategies of War
b. 1990 Clean Air Act
c. 28-hour day
d. Job rotation

44. _________ is a method by which the job performance of an employee is evaluated _________ is a part of career development.

_________s are regular reviews of employee performance within organizations

Generally, the aims of a _________ are to:

- Give feedback on performance to employees.
- Identify employee training needs.
- Document criteria used to allocate organizational rewards.
- Form a basis for personnel decisions: salary increases, promotions, disciplinary actions, etc.
- Provide the opportunity for organizational diagnosis and development.
- Facilitate communication between employee and administraton
- Validate selection techniques and human resource policies to meet federal Equal Employment Opportunity requirements.

A common approach to assessing performance is to use a numerical or scalar rating system whereby managers are asked to score an individual against a number of objectives/attributes. In some companies, employees receive assessments from their manager, peers, subordinates and customers while also performing a self assessment.

a. Performance appraisal
b. Human resource management
c. Progressive discipline
d. Personnel management

45. _________ describes the situation when output from (or information about the result of) an event or phenomenon in the past will influence the same event/phenomenon in the present or future. When an event is part of a chain of cause-and-effect that forms a circuit or loop, then the event is said to 'feed back' into itself.

_________ is also a synonym for:

- _________ signal; the information about the initial event that is the basis for subsequent modification of the event.
- _________ loop; the causal path that leads from the initial generation of the _________ signal to the subsequent modification of the event.

_________ is a mechanism, process or signal that is looped back to control a system within itself. Such a loop is called a _________ loop.

a. 1990 Clean Air Act
b. Feedback loop
c. Positive feedback
d. Feedback

46. In finance, an _________ is a contract between a buyer and a seller that gives the buyer the right--but not the obligation--to buy or to sell a particular asset (the underlying asset) at a later day at an agreed price. In return for granting the _________, the seller collects a payment (the premium) from the buyer. A call _________ gives the buyer the right to buy the underlying asset; a put _________ gives the buyer of the _________ the right to sell the underlying asset.

a. A Stake in the Outcome
b. AAAI
c. A4e
d. Option

47. In economics and sociology, an _________ is any factor (financial or non-financial) that enables or motivates a particular course of action, or counts as a reason for preferring one choice to the alternatives. It is an expectation that encourages people to behave in a certain way. Since human beings are purposeful creatures, the study of _________ structures is central to the study of all economic activity (both in terms of individual decision-making and in terms of co-operation and competition within a larger institutional structure.)

a. A Stake in the Outcome
b. AAAI
c. Incentive
d. A4e

48. _________ is subcontracting a process, such as product design or manufacturing, to a third-party company. The decision to outsource is often made in the interest of lowering cost or making better use of time and energy costs, redirecting or conserving energy directed at the competencies of a particular business, or to make more efficient use of land, labor, capital, (information) technology and resources. _________ became part of the business lexicon during the 1980s.

a. Unemployment insurance
b. Operant conditioning
c. Opinion leadership
d. Outsourcing

49. _________ is the act by an employer of terminating employment. Though such a decision can be made by an employer for a variety of reasons, ranging from an economic downturn to performance-related problems on the part of the employee, being fired has a strong stigma in many cultures. To be fired, as opposed to quitting voluntarily (or being laid off), is often perceived as being the employee's fault, and is therefore considered to be disgraceful and a sign of failure.

a. Layoff
b. Severance package
c. Termination of employment
d. Firing

50. _________ is the temporary suspension or permanent termination of employment of an employee or (more commonly) a group of employees for business reasons, such as the decision that certain positions are no longer necessary or a business slow-down or interruption in work. Originally the term '_________' referred exclusively to a temporary interruption in work, as when factory work cyclically falls off. However, in recent times the term can also refer to the permanent elimination of a position.

a. Wrongful dismissal
b. Termination of employment
c. Retirement
d. Layoff

51. In employment law, _________ refers to a situation where employees in a workplace are subject to a pattern of exposure to unwanted sexual behavior from persons other than an employee's direct supervisor where supervisors or managers take no steps to discourage or discontinue such behavior. It is distinguished from 'quid pro quo' sexual harassment, where a direct supervisor seeks sexual favors in return for something within the supervisor's powers, such as threatening to fire someone, or offering them a raise. Quid pro quo has been recognized as actionable for decades, but hostile environment has only been recognized as an actionable behavior since the late 1980s as courts have made findings that the loss of employment or constructive dismissal has been caused by such behavior.

a. Hostile environment sexual harassment
b. Maturity of Organizations and Business Excellence - The Four-Phase Model
c. Groups decision making
d. STAR

52. _________ indicates a more-or-less equal exchange or substitution of goods or services. English speakers often use the term to mean 'a favour for a favour' and the phrases with almost identical meaning include: 'what for what,' 'give and take,' 'tit for tat', 'this for that', and 'you scratch my back, and I'll scratch yours'.

In legal usage, _________ indicates that an item or a service has been traded in return for something of value, usually when the propriety or equity of the transaction is in question.

a. 1990 Clean Air Act
b. 28-hour day
c. Quid pro quo
d. 33 Strategies of War

53. The _________ refers to a cognitive bias whereby the perception of a particular trait is influenced by the perception of the former traits in a sequence of interpretations.

Edward L. Thorndike was the first to support the _________ with empirical research. In a psychology study published in 1920, Thorndike asked commanding officers to rate their soldiers; Thorndike found high cross-correlation between all positive and all negative traits.

a. Distinction bias
b. Cognitive biases
c. Sunk costs
d. Halo effect

54. The _________ is the labour pool in employment. It is generally used to describe those working for a single company or industry, but can also apply to a geographic region like a city, country, state, etc. The term generally excludes the employers or management, and implies those involved in manual labour.

a. Workforce
b. Pink-collar worker
c. Work-life balance
d. Division of labour

55. _________ is a term defined by the Oxford English Dictionary as an individual's 'course or progress through life '. It is usually considered to pertain to remunerative work (and sometimes also formal education.)

The etymology of the term is somewhat ironic in that it comes from the Latin word carrera, which means race .

a. Spatial mismatch
b. Career planning
c. Nursing shortage
d. Career

56. As defined by Richard Beckhard, _________ is a planned, top-down, organization-wide effort to increase the organization's effectiveness and health. _________ is achieved through interventions in the organization's 'processes,' using behavioural science knowledge. According to Warren Bennis, _________ is a complex strategy intended to change the beliefs, attitudes, values, and structure of organizations so that they can better adapt to new technologies, markets, and challenges.

a. Organizational development
b. Organizational culture
c. Organizational structure
d. Informal organization

57. In the field of human resource management, _________ is the field concerned with organizational activity aimed at bettering the performance of individuals and groups in organizational settings. It has been known by several names, including employee development, human resource development, and learning and development.

Harrison observes that the name was endlessly debated by the Chartered Institute of Personnel and Development during its review of professional standards in 1999/2000.

a. Performance appraisal
b. Training and development
c. Revolving door syndrome
d. Person specification

58. An _________ is a situation that will often involve an apparent conflict between moral imperatives, in which to obey one would result in transgressing another. This is also called an ethical paradox since in moral philosophy, paradox plays a central role in ethics debates. For instance, an ethical admonition to 'love thy neighbour as thy self' is not always just in contrast with, but sometimes in contradiction to an armed neighbour actively trying to kill you: if he or she succeeds, you will not be able to love him or her.

a. A4e
b. AAAI
c. Ethical dilemma
d. A Stake in the Outcome

1. The term '_________' refers to the concept of collecting information and attempting to spot a pattern in the information. In some fields of study, the term '_________' has more formally-defined meanings.

In project management _________ is a mathematical technique that uses historical results to predict future outcome.

a. Stepwise regression
b. Trend analysis
c. Least squares
d. Regression analysis

2. _________ or _________ data refers to selected population characteristics as used in government, marketing or opinion research, or the _________ profiles used in such research. Note the distinction from the term 'demography' Commonly-used _________s include race, age, income, disabilities, mobility (in terms of travel time to work or number of vehicles available), educational attainment, home ownership, employment status, and even location.

a. Abraham Harold Maslow
b. Affiliation
c. Adam Smith
d. Demographic

3. _________ is the strategic and coherent approach to the management of an organisation's most valued assets - the people working there who individually and collectively contribute to the achievement of the objectives of the business. The terms '_________' and 'human resources' (HR) have largely replaced the term 'personnel management' as a description of the processes involved in managing people in organizations. In simple sense, _________ means employing people, developing their resources, utilizing, maintaining and compensating their services in tune with the job and organizational requirement.

a. Progressive discipline
b. Revolving door syndrome
c. Job knowledge
d. Human resource management

4. The 'business case for _________', theorizes that in a global marketplace, a company that employs a diverse workforce (both men and women, people of many generations, people from ethnically and racially diverse backgrounds etc.) is better able to understand the demographics of the marketplace it serves and is thus better equipped to thrive in that marketplace than a company that has a more limited range of employee demographics.

An additional corollary suggests that a company that supports the _________ of its workforce can also improve employee satisfaction, productivity and retention.

a. Kanban
b. Trademark
c. Virtual team
d. Diversity

5. _________ is a theory that describes decisions between alternatives that involve risk, i.e. alternatives with uncertain outcomes, where the probabilities are known. The model is descriptive: it tries to model real-life choices, rather than optimal decisions.

_________ was developed by Daniel Kahneman, professor at Princeton University's Department of Psychology, and Amos Tversky in 1979 as a psychologically realistic alternative to expected utility theory.

a. 1990 Clean Air Act
b. Loss aversion
c. Mental accounting
d. Prospect theory

6. _________ is the process of comparing the cost, cycle time, productivity, or quality of a specific process or method to another that is widely considered to be an industry standard or best practice. Essentially, _________ provides a snapshot of the performance of your business and helps you understand where you are in relation to a particular standard. The result is often a business case for making changes in order to make improvements.

a. Cost leadership
b. Competitive heterogeneity
c. Complementors
d. Benchmarking

7. In economics and sociology, an _________ is any factor (financial or non-financial) that enables or motivates a particular course of action, or counts as a reason for preferring one choice to the alternatives. It is an expectation that encourages people to behave in a certain way. Since human beings are purposeful creatures, the study of _________ structures is central to the study of all economic activity (both in terms of individual decision-making and in terms of co-operation and competition within a larger institutional structure.)

a. Incentive
b. A4e
c. A Stake in the Outcome
d. AAAI

8. _________. The objective of OD is to improve the organization's capacity to handle its internal and external functioning and relationships. This would include such things as improved interpersonal and group processes, more effective communication, enhanced ability to cope with organizational problems of all kinds, more effective decision processes, more appropriate leadership style, improved skill in dealing with destructive conflict, and higher levels of trust and cooperation among organizational members.

a. Organizational structure
b. Organizational development
c. Industrial relations
d. Improved Organizational Performance

9. _________ refers to the long-term management of intractable conflicts. It is the label for the variety of ways by which people handle grievances--standing up for what they consider to be right and against what they consider to be wrong. Those ways include such diverse phenomena as gossip, ridicule, lynching, terrorism, warfare, feuding, genocide, law, mediation, and avoidance.

a. 28-hour day
b. Conflict management
c. 33 Strategies of War
d. 1990 Clean Air Act

10. _________ is a broad label that refers to any individuals or households that use goods and services generated within the economy. The concept of a _________ is used in different contexts, so that the usage and significance of the term may vary.

Typically when business people and economists talk of _________s they are talking about person as _________, an aggregated commodity item with little individuality other than that expressed in the buy/not-buy decision.

a. 33 Strategies of War
b. 1990 Clean Air Act
c. 28-hour day
d. Consumer

11. _________ is one of five major domains of personality discovered by psychologists. Openness involves active imagination, aesthetic sensitivity, attentiveness to inner feelings, preference for variety, and intellectual curiosity. A great deal of psychometric research has demonstrated that these qualities are statistically correlated.

a. Openness to experience
b. Introversion
c. Extraversion
d. Introverts

12. The _________ captures an expanded spectrum of values and criteria for measuring organizational success: economic, ecological and social. With the ratification of the United Nations and ICLEI _________ standard for urban and community accounting in early 2007, this became the dominant approach to public sector full cost accounting. Similar UN standards apply to natural capital and human capital measurement to assist in measurements required by _________, e.g. the ecoBudget standard for reporting ecological footprint.

a. Triple bottom line
b. 33 Strategies of War
c. 28-hour day
d. 1990 Clean Air Act

13. _________ plant, and equipment, is a term used in accountancy for assets and property which cannot easily be converted into cash. This can be compared with current assets such as cash or bank accounts, which are described as liquid assets. In most cases, only tangible assets are referred to as fixed.

a. 28-hour day
b. 33 Strategies of War
c. Fixed asset
d. 1990 Clean Air Act

14. In business and accounting, _________s are everything of value that is owned by a person or company. Any property or object of value that one possesses, usually considered as applicable to the payment of one's debts is considered an _________. Simplistically stated, _________s are things of value that can be readily converted into cash.

a. A4e
b. A Stake in the Outcome
c. AAAI
d. Asset

15. The process of _________ involves the introduction of a good or service that is new or substantially improved. This includes, but is not limited to, improvements in functional characteristics, technical abilities, or ease of use.

a. Job enlargement
b. Service-profit chain
c. Letter of resignation
d. Product innovation

16. _________ generally refers to a list of all planned expenses and revenues. It is a plan for saving and spending. A _________ is an important concept in microeconomics, which uses a _________ line to illustrate the trade-offs between two or more goods.

a. 28-hour day
b. 1990 Clean Air Act
c. 33 Strategies of War
d. Budget

17. An _________ is a person who has possession of an enterprise and assumes significant accountability for the inherent risks and the outcome. It is an ambitious leader who combines land, labor, and capital to create and market new goods or services. The term is a loanword from French and was first defined by the Irish economist Richard Cantillon.

a. A4e
b. AAAI
c. A Stake in the Outcome
d. Entrepreneur

18. _________ is an idea in the field of Organizational studies and management which describes the psychology, attitudes, experiences, beliefs and Values (personal and cultural values) of an organization. It has been defined as 'the specific collection of values and norms that are shared by people and groups in an organization and that control the way they interact with each other and with stakeholders outside the organization.'

This definition continues to explain organizational values also known as 'beliefs and ideas about what kinds of goals members of an organization should pursue and ideas about the appropriate kinds or standards of behavior organizational members should use to achieve these goals. From organizational values develop organizational norms, guidelines or expectations that prescribe appropriate kinds of behavior by employees in particular situations and control the behavior of organizational members towards one another.'

_________ is not the same as corporate culture.

a. Organizational development
b. Organizational effectiveness
c. Union shop
d. Organizational culture

19. The phrase _________, according to the Organization for Economic Co-operation and Development, refers to 'creative work undertaken on a systematic basis in order to increase the stock of knowledge, including knowledge of man, culture and society, and the use of this stock of knowledge to devise new applications [sic]'

New product design and development is more than often a crucial factor in the survival of a company. In an industry that is fast changing, firms must continually revise their design and range of products. This is necessary due to continuous technology change and development as well as other competitors and the changing preference of customers.

a. Research and development
b. 28-hour day
c. 33 Strategies of War
d. 1990 Clean Air Act

20. _________ can be regarded as an outcome of mental processes (cognitive process) leading to the selection of a course of action among several alternatives. Every _________ process produces a final choice. The output can be an action or an opinion of choice.

a. Decision making
b. 28-hour day
c. 33 Strategies of War
d. 1990 Clean Air Act

21. _________ of the learning curve effect and the closely related experience curve effect express the relationship between equations for experience and efficiency or between efficiency gains and investment in the effort. The experience of 'learning curves' was first observed by the 19th Century German psychologist Hermann Ebbinghaus according to the difficulty of memorizing varying numbers of verbal stimuli, and subsequent learning about the complex processes of learning are discussed in the

.

The rule used for representing the learning curve effect states that the more times a task has been performed, the less time will be required on each subsequent iteration.

a. Distribution
b. Point biserial correlation coefficient
c. Models
d. Spatial Decision Support Systems

22. _________-model (SCOR(r)) is a process reference model developed by the management consulting firm PRTM and AMR Research and endorsed by the Supply-Chain Council (SCC) as the cross-industry de facto standard diagnostic tool for supply chain management. SCOR enables users to address, improve, and communicate supply chain management practices within and between all interested parties in the Extended Enterprise.

SCOR(r) is a management tool, spanning from the supplier's supplier to the customer's customer. The model has been developed by the members of the Council on a volunteer basis to describe the business activities associated with all phases of satisfying a customer's demand.

a. Supply Chain Risk Management
b. Delayed differentiation
c. Supply chain management software
d. Supply-Chain Operations Reference

1. _________ means increasing the scope of a job through extending the range of its job duties and responsibilities. This contradicts the principles of specialisation and the division of labour whereby work is divided into small units, each of which is performed repetitively by an individual worker. Some motivational theories suggest that the boredom and alienation caused by the division of labour can actually cause efficiency to fall.

a. Centralization
b. Job enlargement
c. Delayering
d. Mock interview

2. _________ is a mathematical science pertaining to the collection, analysis, interpretation or explanation, and presentation of data. It also provides tools for prediction and forecasting based on data. It is applicable to a wide variety of academic disciplines, from the natural and social sciences to the humanities, government and business.

a. Simple moving average
b. Statistics
c. Failure rate
d. Location parameter

3. _________ refers to techniques, processes and tools for organizing and coordinating a group of individuals working towards a common goal--i.e. a team.

Several well-known approaches to _________ have come out of academic work. Examples include the Belbin Team Inventory by Meredith Belbin, a method to identify the different types of personalities within teams, and Ken Blanchard's description of 'High Performing Teams'.

a. 33 Strategies of War
b. 28-hour day
c. Team management
d. 1990 Clean Air Act

4. _________ is one of the managerial functions like planning, organizing, staffing and directing. It is an important function because it helps to check the errors and to take the corrective action so that deviation from standards are minimized and stated goals of the organization are achieved in desired manner.According to modern concepts, _________ is a foreseeing action whereas earlier concept of _________ was used only when errors were detected. _________ in management means setting standards, measuring actual performance and taking corrective action.

a. Schedule of reinforcement
b. Decision tree pruning
c. Control
d. Turnover

5. _________ can be regarded as an outcome of mental processes (cognitive process) leading to the selection of a course of action among several alternatives. Every _________ process produces a final choice. The output can be an action or an opinion of choice.

a. 1990 Clean Air Act
b. 28-hour day
c. Decision making
d. 33 Strategies of War

6. In decision theory and estimation theory, the _________ of an estimator, $\hat{\theta}$, of an unknown parameter of the distribution, θ, is the expected value of the loss function

$$R(\theta,\hat{\theta}) = \mathbb{E}_\theta L(\theta,\hat{\theta}) = \int L(\theta,\hat{\theta})\, dP_\theta.$$

where dP_θ is a probability measure parametrized by θ.

- For a scalar parameter θ and a quadratic loss function,

$$L(\theta,\hat{\theta}) = (\theta - \hat{\theta})^2$$

the _________ function becomes the mean squared error of the estimate,

$$R(\theta,\hat{\theta}) = E_\theta(\theta - \hat{\theta})^2$$

- In density estimation, the unknown parameter is probability density itself. The loss function is typically chosen to be a norm in an appropriate function space. For example, for L^2 norm,

$$L(f,\hat{f}) = \|f - \hat{f}\|_2^2$$

the _________ function becomes the mean integrated squared error

$$R(f,\hat{f}) = E\|f - \hat{f}\|^2$$

.

a. Risk
b. Risk aversion
c. Linear model
d. Financial modeling

7. _________ is a habitual pattern of absence from a duty or obligation.

Frequent absence from the workplace may be indicative of poor morale or of sick building syndrome. However, many employers have implemented absence policies which make no distinction between absences for genuine illness and absence for inappropriate reasons.

a. A Stake in the Outcome
b. A4e
c. Emanation of the state
d. Absenteeism

8. _________ is an uncomfortable feeling caused by holding two contradictory ideas simultaneously. The 'ideas' or 'cognitions' in question may include attitudes and beliefs, and also the awareness of one's behavior. The theory of _________ proposes that people have a motivational drive to reduce dissonance by changing their attitudes, beliefs, and behaviors, or by justifying or rationalizing their attitudes, beliefs, and behaviors.

a. Cognitive dissonance
b. Quantitative psychology
c. Trait theory
d. Cognitive bias

9. _________ describes how content an individual is with his or her job.

The happier people are within their job, the more satisfied they are said to be. _________ is not the same as motivation, although it is clearly linked.

a. Job analysis
b. Human relations
c. Goal-setting theory
d. Job satisfaction

10. In a human resources context, _________ or labor _________ is the rate at which an employer gains and loses employees. Simple ways to describe it are 'how long employees tend to stay' or 'the rate of traffic through the revolving door.' _________ is measured for individual companies and for their industry as a whole. If an employer is said to have a high _________ relative to its competitors, it means that employees of that company have a shorter average tenure than those of other companies in the same industry.

a. Ten year occupational employment projection
b. Turnover
c. Continuous
d. Career portfolios

11. The trait of _________ is a central dimension of human personality. Extraverts (also spelled extroverts) tend to be gregarious, assertive, and interested in seeking out excitement. Introverts, in contrast, tend to be more reserved, less outgoing, and less sociable.

a. AAAI
b. A4e
c. A Stake in the Outcome
d. Extraversion-introversion

12. _________ is one of five major domains of personality discovered by psychologists. Openness involves active imagination, aesthetic sensitivity, attentiveness to inner feelings, preference for variety, and intellectual curiosity. A great deal of psychometric research has demonstrated that these qualities are statistically correlated.

a. Introverts
b. Introversion
c. Extraversion
d. Openness to experience

13. _________ is a term in psychology which refers to a person's belief about what causes the good or bad results in his or her life, either in general or in a specific area such as health or academics. Understanding of the concept was developed by Julian B. Rotter in 1954, and has since become an important aspect of personality studies.

_________ refers to the extent to which individuals believe that they can control events that affect them.

a. Machiavellianism
b. Self-enhancement
c. Social loafing
d. Locus of control

14. _________ occurs when expectant women are fired, not hired, or otherwise discriminated against due to their pregnancy or intention to become pregnant. Common forms of _________ include not being hired due to visible pregnancy or likelihood of becoming pregnant, being fired after informing an employer of one's pregnancy, being fired after maternity leave, and receiving a pay dock due to pregnancy. In the United States, since 1978, employers are legally bound to provide what insurance, leave pay, and additional support that would be bestowed upon any employee with medical leave or disability.

a. 33 Strategies of War
b. Pregnancy Discrimination
c. 1990 Clean Air Act
d. 28-hour day

15. _________ is a set of values based on hard work and diligence. It is also a belief in the moral benefit of work and its ability to enhance character. An example would be the Protestant _________.

a. 33 Strategies of War
b. Work ethic
c. 1990 Clean Air Act
d. 28-hour day

16. In psychology, _________ is a major approach to the study of human personality. Trait theorists are primarily interested in the measurement of traits, which can be defined as habitual patterns of behavior, thought, and emotion. According to this perspective, traits are relatively stable over time, differ among individuals (e.g. some people are outgoing whereas others are shy), and influence behavior.

a. Psychological statistics
b. Psychometrics
c. Cognitive dissonance
d. Trait theory

17. _________ indicates a more-or-less equal exchange or substitution of goods or services. English speakers often use the term to mean 'a favour for a favour' and the phrases with almost identical meaning include: 'what for what,' 'give and take,' 'tit for tat', 'this for that', and 'you scratch my back, and I'll scratch yours'.

In legal usage, _________ indicates that an item or a service has been traded in return for something of value, usually when the propriety or equity of the transaction is in question.

a. 1990 Clean Air Act
b. 33 Strategies of War
c. Quid pro quo
d. 28-hour day

18. _________ is the belief that one is capable of performing in a certain manner to attain certain goals. It is a belief that one has the capabilities to execute the courses of actions required to manage prospective situations. Unlike efficacy, which is the power to produce an effect (in essence, competence), _________ is the belief (whether or not accurate) that one has the power to produce that effect.

a. 1990 Clean Air Act
b. 28-hour day
c. 33 Strategies of War
d. Self-efficacy

19. In psychology, _________ reflects a person's overall evaluation or appraisal of his or her own worth.

_________ encompasses beliefs (for example, 'I am competent/incompetent') and emotions (for example, triumph/despair, pride/shame.) Behavior may reflect _________

a. Self-esteem
b. 1990 Clean Air Act
c. 28-hour day
d. 33 Strategies of War

20. _________ is unwelcome harassment of a sexual nature, or based upon the receiving party's sex or gender. In some contexts or circumstances, _________ may be illegal. It includes a range of behavior from seemingly mild transgressions and annoyances to actual sexual abuse or sexual assault.

a. 1990 Clean Air Act
b. Hypernorms
c. 28-hour day
d. Sexual harassment

21. _________ plant, and equipment, is a term used in accountancy for assets and property which cannot easily be converted into cash. This can be compared with current assets such as cash or bank accounts, which are described as liquid assets. In most cases, only tangible assets are referred to as fixed.

a. Fixed asset
b. 28-hour day
c. 1990 Clean Air Act
d. 33 Strategies of War

22. The _________ refers to a cognitive bias whereby the perception of a particular trait is influenced by the perception of the former traits in a sequence of interpretations.

Edward L. Thorndike was the first to support the _________ with empirical research. In a psychology study published in 1920, Thorndike asked commanding officers to rate their soldiers; Thorndike found high cross-correlation between all positive and all negative traits.

a. Sunk costs
b. Halo effect
c. Cognitive biases
d. Distinction bias

23. In business and accounting, _________s are everything of value that is owned by a person or company. Any property or object of value that one possesses, usually considered as applicable to the payment of one's debts is considered an _________. Simplistically stated, _________s are things of value that can be readily converted into cash.

a. A Stake in the Outcome
b. A4e
c. AAAI
d. Asset

24. A _________ is a compensation, usually financial, received by a worker in exchange for their labor.

Compensation in terms of _________s is given to worker and compensation in terms of salary is given to employees. Compensation is a monetary benefits given to employees in returns of the services provided by them.

a. Wage
b. State Compensation Insurance Fund
c. Performance-related pay
d. Profit-sharing agreement

25. Income disparity or _________ is a term used to describe inequities and asymmetry in the distribution of wealth and income between socio-economic groups within society. The term also has many other definitions:

Common examples include:

- The income gap between the wealthy and the poor.
- lower average income for females than males

In the context of economic inequality, gender gap generally refers to the differences in the wages of men and women, or boys and girls. There is a debate to what extent this is the result of gender differences, lifestyle choices (e.g., number of hours worked), or because of discrimination.

A United Nations report found that women working in manufacturing earned the following percentages in relation to men in 2003.

a. Division of labour
b. Workforce
c. Quality of working life
d. Wage gap

26. The _________ refers to situations in which students perform better than other students simply because they are expected to do so. The effect is named after George Bernard Shaw's play Pygmalion, in which a professor makes a bet that he can teach a poor flower girl to speak and act like an upper-class lady, and is successful.

The _________ requires a student to internalize the expectations of their superiors.

a. Confirmation bias
b. Distinction bias
c. Halo effect
d. Pygmalion effect

27. A _________ is a prediction that directly or indirectly causes itself to become true, by the very terms of the prophecy itself, due to positive feedback between belief and behavior. Although examples of such prophecies can be found in literature as far back as ancient Greece and ancient India, it is 20th-century sociologist Robert K. Merton who is credited with coining the expression '_________' and formalizing its structure and consequences. In his book Social Theory and Social Structure, Merton gives as a feature of the _________:

In other words, a prophecy declared as truth when it is actually false may sufficiently influence people, either through fear or logical confusion, so that their reactions ultimately fulfill the once-false prophecy.

a. 28-hour day
b. 1990 Clean Air Act
c. 33 Strategies of War
d. Self-fulfilling prophecy

28. A _________ occurs when people attribute their successes to internal or personal factors but attribute their failures to situational factors beyond their control. The _________ can be seen in the common human tendency to take credit for success but to deny responsibility for failure. It may also manifest itself as a tendency for people to evaluate ambiguous information in a way that is beneficial to their interests.

a. Halo effect
b. Fundamental attribution error
c. Pygmalion effect
d. Self-serving bias

29. In organizational development (OD), _________ is the application of Socio-Technical Systems principles and techniques to the humanization of work.

The aims of _________ to improved job satisfaction, to improved through-put, to improved quality and to reduced employee problems, e.g., grievances, absenteeism.

Under scientific management people would be directed by reason and the problems of industrial unrest would be appropriately (i.e., scientifically) addressed.

a. Graduate recruitment
b. Path-goal theory
c. Management process
d. Work design

30. _________ Management is the succession of strategies used by management as a product goes through its _________. The conditions in which a product is sold changes over time and must be managed as it moves through its succession of stages.

The _________ goes through many phases, involves many professional disciplines, and requires many skills, tools and processes.

a. Golden handshake
b. Strategic Alliance
c. Job hunting
d. Product life cycle

31. '_________ is a conflict among the roles corresponding to two or more statuses.'

_________ is a special form of social conflict that takes place when one is forced to take on two different and incompatible roles at the same time. Consider the example of a doctor who is himself a patient, or who must decide whether he should be present for his daughter's birthday party (in his role as 'father') or attend an ailing patient (as 'doctor'.) (Also compare the psychological concept of cognitive dissonance.)

a. Social network analysis
b. Soft skill
c. Self-disclosure
d. Role conflict

32. A _________ is a formal relationship between two or more parties to pursue a set of agreed upon goals or to meet a critical business need while remaining independent organizations.

Partners may provide the _________ with resources such as products, distribution channels, manufacturing capability, project funding, capital equipment, knowledge, expertise, or intellectual property. The alliance is a cooperation or collaboration which aims for a synergy where each partner hopes that the benefits from the alliance will be greater than those from individual efforts.

a. Golden parachute
b. Farmshoring
c. Process automation
d. Strategic alliance

33. In economics, _________ is the desire to own something and the ability to pay for it. The term _________ signifies the ability or the willingness to buy a particular commodity at a given point of time.
a. 28-hour day
b. 1990 Clean Air Act
c. 33 Strategies of War
d. Demand

34. In finance, an _________ is a contract between a buyer and a seller that gives the buyer the right--but not the obligation--to buy or to sell a particular asset (the underlying asset) at a later day at an agreed price. In return for granting the _________, the seller collects a payment (the premium) from the buyer. A call _________ gives the buyer the right to buy the underlying asset; a put _________ gives the buyer of the _________ the right to sell the underlying asset.
a. Option
b. A Stake in the Outcome
c. A4e
d. AAAI

35. _________ refers to various methodologies for analyzing the requirements of a job.

The general purpose of _________ is to document the requirements of a job and the work performed. Job and task analysis is performed as a basis for later improvements, including: definition of a job domain; describing a job; developing performance appraisals, selection systems, promotion criteria, training needs assessment, and compensation plans.

a. Hersey-Blanchard situational theory
b. Work design
c. Management process
d. Job analysis

36. _________ , often measured as an _________ Quotient (EQ), is a term that describes the ability, capacity, skill or (in the case of the trait _________ model) a self-perceived ability, to identify, assess, and manage the emotions of one's self, of others, and of groups. Different models have been proposed for the definition of _________ and disagreement exists as to how the term should be used. Despite these disagreements, which are often highly technical, the ability _________ and trait _________ models (but not the mixed models) are enjoying considerable support in the literature and have successful applications in many different domains.

a. A Stake in the Outcome
b. Emotional intelligence
c. AAAI
d. A4e

37. A _________ is a list of the general tasks and responsibilities of a position. Typically, it also includes to whom the position reports, specifications such as the qualifications needed by the person in the job, salary range for the position, etc. A _________ is usually developed by conducting a job analysis, which includes examining the tasks and sequences of tasks necessary to perform the job.

a. Recruitment
b. Recruitment Process Insourcing
c. Recruitment advertising
d. Job description

38. In business and engineering, new _________ is the term used to describe the complete process of bringing a new product or service to market. There are two parallel paths involved in the NProduct development process: one involves the idea generation, product design, and detail engineering; the other involves market research and marketing analysis. Companies typically see new _________ as the first stage in generating and commercializing new products within the overall strategic process of product life cycle management used to maintain or grow their market share.

a. 1990 Clean Air Act
b. 33 Strategies of War
c. 28-hour day
d. Product development

39. _________ is the strategic and coherent approach to the management of an organisation's most valued assets - the people working there who individually and collectively contribute to the achievement of the objectives of the business. The terms '_________' and 'human resources' (HR) have largely replaced the term 'personnel management' as a description of the processes involved in managing people in organizations. In simple sense, _________ means employing people, developing their resources, utilizing, maintaining and compensating their services in tune with the job and organizational requirement.

a. Progressive discipline
b. Revolving door syndrome
c. Job knowledge
d. Human resource management

1. The 'business case for _________', theorizes that in a global marketplace, a company that employs a diverse workforce (both men and women, people of many generations, people from ethnically and racially diverse backgrounds etc.) is better able to understand the demographics of the marketplace it serves and is thus better equipped to thrive in that marketplace than a company that has a more limited range of employee demographics.

An additional corollary suggests that a company that supports the _________ of its workforce can also improve employee satisfaction, productivity and retention.

a. Kanban
b. Diversity
c. Virtual team
d. Trademark

2. _________ is a variable work schedule, in contrast to traditional work arrangements requiring employees to work a standard 9am to 5pm day. Under _________, there is typically a core period of the day when employees are expected to be at work (for example, between 11 am and 3pm), while the rest of the working day is 'flexitime', in which employees can choose when they work, subject to achieving total daily, weekly or monthly hours in the region of what the employer expects, and subject to the necessary work being done.

A _________ policy allows staff to determine when they will work, while a flexplace policy allows staff to determine where they will work.

a. Flextime
b. Certificate of Incorporation
c. Bennett Amendment
d. Fiduciary

3. _________, e-commuting, e-work, telework, working from home (WFH), or working at home (WAH) is a work arrangement in which employees enjoy flexibility in working location and hours. In other words, the daily commute to a central place of work is replaced by telecommunication links. Many work from home, while others, occasionally also referred to as nomad workers or web commuters utilize mobile telecommunications technology to work from coffee shops or myriad other locations.

a. Telecommuting
b. 33 Strategies of War
c. 1990 Clean Air Act
d. 28-hour day

4. The legal _________ varies from nation to nation. The weekend is a part of the week usually lasting one or two days in which most paid workers do not work.

In Muslim-majority countries the legal work week in the Middle East is typically either Saturday through Wednesday , Saturday through Thursday or Sunday through Thursday as in Egypt.

a. Working Time Directive
b. Day One Christian Ministries
c. Business day
d. Workweek

5. Maslow's _________ is a theory in psychology, proposed by Abraham Maslow in his 1943 paper A Theory of Human Motivation, which he subsequently extended to include his observations of humans' innate curiosity.

Maslow's _________ is predetermined in order of importance. It is often depicted as a pyramid consisting of five levels: the lowest level is associated with physiological needs, while the uppermost level is associated with self-actualization needs, particularly those related to identity and purpose. Deficiency needs must be met first. Once these are met, seeking to satisfy growth needs drives personal growth. The higher needs in this hierarchy only come into focus when the lower needs in the pyramid are met.

a. 33 Strategies of War
b. 28-hour day
c. 1990 Clean Air Act
d. Hierarchy of needs

6. _________ is a term that has been used in various psychology theories, often in slightly different ways (e.g., Goldstein, Maslow, Rogers.) The term was originally introduced by the organismic theorist Kurt Goldstein for the motive to realise all of one's potentialities. In his view, it is the master motive--indeed, the only real motive a person has, all others being merely manifestations of it.

a. 33 Strategies of War
b. 28-hour day
c. Self-actualization
d. 1990 Clean Air Act

7. _________ are job factors that can cause dissatisfaction if missing but do not necessarily motivate employees if increased.

_________ have mostly to do with the job environment. These factors are important or notable only when they are lacking.

a. Hygiene factors
b. Work system
c. Split shift
d. Work-at-home scheme

8. _________ describes how content an individual is with his or her job.

The happier people are within their job, the more satisfied they are said to be. _________ is not the same as motivation, although it is clearly linked.

a. Human relations
b. Job analysis
c. Goal-setting theory
d. Job satisfaction

9. _________ is a term coined by Deborah E. Meyerson used to describe corporate professionals who work toward positive change in both their work environment and the way their companies conduct business -- often taking 'radical' action that is just short of getting them fired.

In her book, _________: How Everyday Leaders Inspire Change at Work (Harvard Business School Press), Meyerson describes employees who believe and work toward creating adaptive, family-friendly, and socially responsible workplaces.

_________ are quiet leaders that act as catalysts for new ideas, alternative perspectives, and organizational learning and change -- and balance company conformity with individual rebellion.

a. 33 Strategies of War
b. 28-hour day
c. 1990 Clean Air Act
d. Tempered radicals

10. _________ was developed by Frederick Herzberg, a psychologist who found that job satisfaction and job dissatisfaction acted independently of each other. _________ states that there are certain factors in the workplace that cause job satisfaction, while a separate set of factors cause dissatisfaction.

a. 1990 Clean Air Act
b. Two-factor theory
c. Need for Achievement
d. Need for power

11. _________ is about the mental processes regarding choice, or choosing. It explains the processes that an individual undergoes to make choices. In organizational behavior study, _________ is a motivation theory first proposed by Victor Vroom of the Yale School of Management.

a. Expectancy theory
b. AAAI
c. A4e
d. A Stake in the Outcome

12. _________ is an uncomfortable feeling caused by holding two contradictory ideas simultaneously. The 'ideas' or 'cognitions' in question may include attitudes and beliefs, and also the awareness of one's behavior. The theory of _________ proposes that people have a motivational drive to reduce dissonance by changing their attitudes, beliefs, and behaviors, or by justifying or rationalizing their attitudes, beliefs, and behaviors.

a. Cognitive dissonance
b. Trait theory
c. Quantitative psychology
d. Cognitive bias

13. The _________ of 1977 (15 U.S.C. Â§Â§ 78dd-1, et seq.) is a United States federal law known primarily for two of its main provisions, one that addresses accounting transparency requirements under the Securities Exchange Act of 1934 and another concerning bribery of foreign officials.

a. Social Security Act of 1965
b. Foreign Corrupt Practices Act
c. Meritor Savings Bank v. Vinson
d. Limited liability

14. In decision theory and estimation theory, the _________ of an estimator, $\hat{\theta}$, of an unknown parameter of the distribution, θ, is the expected value of the loss function

$$R(\theta,\hat{\theta}) = \mathbb{E}_\theta L(\theta,\hat{\theta}) = \int L(\theta,\hat{\theta})\, dP_\theta.$$

where dP_θ is a probability measure parametrized by θ.

- For a scalar parameter θ and a quadratic loss function,

$$L(\theta, \hat{\theta}) = (\theta - \hat{\theta})^2$$

the _________ function becomes the mean squared error of the estimate,

$$R(\theta, \hat{\theta}) = E_\theta(\theta - \hat{\theta})^2$$

- In density estimation, the unknown parameter is probability density itself. The loss function is typically chosen to be a norm in an appropriate function space. For example, for L^2 norm,

$$L(f, \hat{f}) = \|f - \hat{f}\|_2^2$$

the _________ function becomes the mean integrated squared error

$$R(f, \hat{f}) = E\|f - \hat{f}\|^2$$

.

a. Risk aversion
b. Financial modeling
c. Risk
d. Linear model

15. The _________ is the Cabinet department of the United States government concerned with promoting economic growth. It was originally created as the _________ and Labor on February 14, 1903. It was subsequently renamed to the Department of Commerce on March 4, 1913, and its bureaus and agencies specializing in labor were transferred to the new Department of Labor.

a. A Stake in the Outcome
b. A4e
c. AAAI
d. United States Department of Commerce

16. _________ attempts to explain relational satisfaction in terms of perceptions of fair/unfair distributions of resources within interpersonal relationships. _________ is considered as one of the justice theories, It was first developed in 1962 by John Stacey Adams, a workplace and behavioral psychologist, who asserted that employees seek to maintain equity between the inputs that they bring to a job and the outcomes that they receive from it against the perceived inputs and outcomes of others (Adams, 1965.) The belief is that people value fair treatment which causes them to be motivated to keep the fairness maintained within the relationships of their co-workers and the organization.

a. A Stake in the Outcome
b. A4e
c. AAAI
d. Equity theory

17. _________ has become one of the most popular theories in organizational psychology.

Goal setting has been a formula used for acheivement since the early 1800s. The form and pattern has cahanged drastically over the years and there is still much debate as to what is the most efective pattern to follow.

a. Human relations
b. Corporate Culture
c. Goal-setting theory
d. Job satisfaction

18. _________ is the use of empirically demonstrated behavior change techniques to improve behavior, such as altering an individual's behaviors and reactions to stimuli through positive and negative reinforcement of adaptive behavior and/or the reduction of maladaptive behavior through punishment and/or therapy.

The first use of the term _________ appears to have been by Edward Thorndike in 1911

a. 33 Strategies of War
b. 28-hour day
c. 1990 Clean Air Act
d. Behavior modification

19. _________ is the use of consequences to modify the occurrence and form of behavior. _________ is distinguished from classical conditioning (also called respondent conditioning, or Pavlovian conditioning) in that _________ deals with the modification of 'voluntary behavior' or operant behavior. Operant behavior 'operates' on the environment and is maintained by its consequences, while classical conditioning deals with the conditioning of respondent behaviors which are elicited by antecedent conditions.

a. Outsourcing
b. Unemployment insurance
c. Operant conditioning
d. Occupational Safety and Health Administration

20. _________ refers to the movement of cash into or out of a business or financial product. It is usually measured during a specified, finite period of time. Measurement of _________ can be used

- to determine a project's rate of return or value. The time of _________s into and out of projects are used as inputs in financial models such as internal rate of return, and net present value.
- to determine problems with a business's liquidity. Being profitable does not necessarily mean being liquid. A company can fail because of a shortage of cash, even while profitable.
- as an alternate measure of a business's profits when it is believed that accrual accounting concepts do not represent economic realities. For example, a company may be notionally profitable but generating little operational cash (as may be the case for a company that barters its products rather than selling for cash.) In such a case, the company may be deriving additional operating cash by issuing shares evaluating default risk, re-investment requirements, etc.

_________ is a generic term used differently depending on the context. It may be defined by users for their own purposes.

a. Gross profit
b. Gross profit margin
c. Sweat equity
d. Cash flow

21. In operant conditioning, _________ occurs when an event following a response causes an increase in the probability of that response occurring in the future. Response strength can be assessed by measures such as the frequency with which the response is made (for example, a pigeon may peck a key more times in the session), or the speed with which it is made (for example, a rat may run a maze faster.) The environment change contingent upon the response is called a reinforcer.

a. Historiometry
b. Diminishing Manufacturing Sources and Material Shortages
c. Meetings, Incentives, Conferences, and Exhibitions
d. Reinforcement

22. _________ refers to training in different ways to improve overall performance. It takes advantage of the particular effectiveness of each training method, while at the same time attempting to neglect the shortcomings of that method by combining it with other methods that address its weaknesses.

Cross training is employee-employer field means, training employees to do one another's work.

a. Cross-training
b. 33 Strategies of War
c. 1990 Clean Air Act
d. 28-hour day

23. In organizational development (OD), _________ is the application of Socio-Technical Systems principles and techniques to the humanization of work.

The aims of _________ to improved job satisfaction, to improved through-put, to improved quality and to reduced employee problems, e.g., grievances, absenteeism.

Under scientific management people would be directed by reason and the problems of industrial unrest would be appropriately (i.e., scientifically) addressed.

a. Graduate recruitment
b. Management process
c. Path-goal theory
d. Work design

24. _________ means increasing the scope of a job through extending the range of its job duties and responsibilities. This contradicts the principles of specialisation and the division of labour whereby work is divided into small units, each of which is performed repetitively by an individual worker. Some motivational theories suggest that the boredom and alienation caused by the division of labour can actually cause efficiency to fall.

a. Delayering
b. Mock interview
c. Centralization
d. Job enlargement

25. The _________ captures an expanded spectrum of values and criteria for measuring organizational success: economic, ecological and social. With the ratification of the United Nations and ICLEI _________ standard for urban and community accounting in early 2007, this became the dominant approach to public sector full cost accounting. Similar UN standards apply to natural capital and human capital measurement to assist in measurements required by _________, e.g. the ecoBudget standard for reporting ecological footprint.

a. 1990 Clean Air Act
b. Triple bottom line
c. 33 Strategies of War
d. 28-hour day

26. In mathematical logic, _________ is a valid argument and rule of inference which makes the inference that, if the conjunction A and B is true, then A is true, and B is true.

In formal language:

$$A \wedge B \vdash A$$

or

$$A \wedge B \vdash B$$

The argument has one premise, namely a conjunction, and one often uses _________ in longer arguments to derive one of the conjuncts.

An example in English:

It's raining and it's pouring.

a. Fuzzy logic
b. Validity
c. Simplification
d. 1990 Clean Air Act

27. _________ is an attempt to motivate employees by giving them the opportunity to use the range of their abilities. It is an idea that was developed by the American psychologist Frederick Herzberg in the 1950s. It can be contrasted to job enlargement which simply increases the number of tasks without changing the challenge.

a. Catfish effect
b. Cash cow
c. C-A-K-E
d. Job enrichment

28. _________ , often measured as an _________ Quotient (EQ), is a term that describes the ability, capacity, skill or (in the case of the trait _________ model) a self-perceived ability, to identify, assess, and manage the emotions of one's self, of others, and of groups. Different models have been proposed for the definition of _________ and disagreement exists as to how the term should be used. Despite these disagreements, which are often highly technical, the ability _________ and trait _________ models (but not the mixed models) are enjoying considerable support in the literature and have successful applications in many different domains.

a. A Stake in the Outcome
b. AAAI
c. Emotional intelligence
d. A4e

29. _________-model (SCOR(r)) is a process reference model developed by the management consulting firm PRTM and AMR Research and endorsed by the Supply-Chain Council (SCC) as the cross-industry de facto standard diagnostic tool for supply chain management. SCOR enables users to address, improve, and communicate supply chain management practices within and between all interested parties in the Extended Enterprise.

SCOR(r) is a management tool, spanning from the supplier's supplier to the customer's customer. The model has been developed by the members of the Council on a volunteer basis to describe the business activities associated with all phases of satisfying a customer's demand.

a. Supply chain management software
b. Delayed differentiation
c. Supply Chain Risk Management
d. Supply-Chain Operations Reference

30. A _________ or chief operations officer is a corporate officer responsible for managing the day-to-day activities of the corporation and for operations management (OM.) The _________ is one of the highest-ranking members of an organization's senior management, monitoring the daily operations of the company and reporting to the board of directors and the top executive officer, usually the chief executive officer (CEO.) The _________ is usually an executive or senior officer.

a. Value based pricing
b. Chief operating officer
c. Product innovation
d. Supervisory board

31. _________ is an idea in the field of Organizational studies and management which describes the psychology, attitudes, experiences, beliefs and Values (personal and cultural values) of an organization. It has been defined as 'the specific collection of values and norms that are shared by people and groups in an organization and that control the way they interact with each other and with stakeholders outside the organization.'

This definition continues to explain organizational values also known as 'beliefs and ideas about what kinds of goals members of an organization should pursue and ideas about the appropriate kinds or standards of behavior organizational members should use to achieve these goals. From organizational values develop organizational norms, guidelines or expectations that prescribe appropriate kinds of behavior by employees in particular situations and control the behavior of organizational members towards one another.'

_________ is not the same as corporate culture.

a. Union shop
b. Organizational development
c. Organizational effectiveness
d. Organizational culture

32. _________ is a term describing performance-related pay, most frequently in the context of educational reform. It provides bonuses for workers who perform their jobs better, according to measurable criteria. In the United States, policy makers are divided on whether _________ should be offered to public school teachers, as is commonly the case in the United Kingdom.

a. Real wage
b. Merit pay
c. Performance-related pay
d. Profit-sharing agreement

33. _________. The objective of OD is to improve the organization's capacity to handle its internal and external functioning and relationships. This would include such things as improved interpersonal and group processes, more effective communication, enhanced ability to cope with organizational problems of all kinds, more effective decision processes, more appropriate leadership style, improved skill in dealing with destructive conflict, and higher levels of trust and cooperation among organizational members.

a. Improved Organizational Performance
b. Industrial relations
c. Organizational development
d. Organizational structure

34. Piece work or piecework describes types of employment in which a worker is paid a fixed '_________' for each unit produced or action performed. Piece work is also a form of performance-related pay (Piece rateP) and is the oldest form of performance pay.

In a manufacturing setting, the output of piece work can be measured by the number of physical items (pieces) produced, such as when a garment worker is paid per operational step completed, regardless of the time required.

a. Piecework
b. Scientific management
c. Methods-time measurement
d. Piece rate

35. _________, when used as a special term, refers to various incentive plans introduced by businesses that provide direct or indirect payments to employees that depend on company's profitability in addition to employees' regular salary and bonuses. In publicly traded companies these plans typically amount to allocation of shares to employees.

The _________ plans are based on predetermined economic sharing rules that define the split of gains between the company as a principal and the employee as an agent.

a. Wage
b. Profit sharing
c. Federal Wage System
d. Living wage

36. In finance, an _________ is a contract between a buyer and a seller that gives the buyer the right--but not the obligation--to buy or to sell a particular asset (the underlying asset) at a later day at an agreed price. In return for granting the _________, the seller collects a payment (the premium) from the buyer. A call _________ gives the buyer the right to buy the underlying asset; a put _________ gives the buyer of the _________ the right to sell the underlying asset.

a. A Stake in the Outcome
b. AAAI
c. Option
d. A4e

37. In economics and sociology, an _________ is any factor (financial or non-financial) that enables or motivates a particular course of action, or counts as a reason for preferring one choice to the alternatives. It is an expectation that encourages people to behave in a certain way. Since human beings are purposeful creatures, the study of _________ structures is central to the study of all economic activity (both in terms of individual decision-making and in terms of co-operation and competition within a larger institutional structure.)

a. A Stake in the Outcome
b. Incentive
c. AAAI
d. A4e

38. The general definition of an _________ is an evaluation of a person, organization, system, process, project or product. _________s are performed to ascertain the validity and reliability of information; also to provide an assessment of a system's internal control. The goal of an _________ is to express an opinion on the person / organization/system (etc) in question, under evaluation based on work done on a test basis.

a. Audit
b. Audit committee
c. A Stake in the Outcome
d. Internal control

39. The term _________ refers to a salaried professional or an educated worker who performs semi-professional office, administrative, and sales coordination tasks, as opposed to a blue-collar worker, whose job requires manual labor. 'White-collar work' is an informal term, defined in contrast to 'blue-collar work'.

The term 'white collar' was first used by Upton Sinclair in relation to modern clerical, administrative and management workers during the 1930s.

a. 1990 Clean Air Act
b. 28-hour day
c. 33 Strategies of War
d. White-collar worker

40. _________ is a leadership style that defines as leadership that creates voluble and positive change in the followers. A transformational leader focuses on 'transforming' others to help each other, to look out for each other, be encouraging, harmonious, and look out for the organization as a whole. In this leadership, the leader enhances the motivation, moral and performance of his follower group.

a. Transformational leadership
b. Polynomial conjoint measurement
c. SESAMO
d. Strong-Campbell Interest Inventory

41. An _________ is a situation that will often involve an apparent conflict between moral imperatives, in which to obey one would result in transgressing another. This is also called an ethical paradox since in moral philosophy, paradox plays a central role in ethics debates. For instance, an ethical admonition to 'love thy neighbour as thy self' is not always just in contrast with, but sometimes in contradiction to an armed neighbour actively trying to kill you: if he or she succeeds, you will not be able to love him or her.

a. A Stake in the Outcome
b. AAAI
c. A4e
d. Ethical dilemma

42. _________ is the act by an employer of terminating employment. Though such a decision can be made by an employer for a variety of reasons, ranging from an economic downturn to performance-related problems on the part of the employee, being fired has a strong stigma in many cultures. To be fired, as opposed to quitting voluntarily (or being laid off), is often perceived as being the employee's fault, and is therefore considered to be disgraceful and a sign of failure.

a. Severance package
b. Termination of employment
c. Layoff
d. Firing

43. _________ has been described as the 'process of social influence in which one person can enlist the aid and support of others in the accomplishment of a common task' . A definition more inclusive of followers comes from Alan Keith of Genentech who said '_________ is ultimately about creating a way for people to contribute to making something extraordinary happen.'

_________ is one of the most salient aspects of the organizational context. However, defining _________ has been challenging.

a. Situational leadership
b. 28-hour day
c. Leadership
d. 1990 Clean Air Act

1. _________ is a recursive process where two or more people or organizations work together in an intersection of common goals -- for example, an intellectual endeavor that is creative in nature--by sharing knowledge, learning and building consensus. _________ does not require leadership and can sometimes bring better results through decentralization and egalitarianism. In particular, teams that work collaboratively can obtain greater resources, recognition and reward when facing competition for finite resources._________ is also present in opposing goals exhibiting the notion of adversarial _________, though this is not a common case for using the term.

a. 1990 Clean Air Act
b. Collectivism
c. Collaboration
d. 28-hour day

2. _________ refers to the long-term management of intractable conflicts. It is the label for the variety of ways by which people handle grievances--standing up for what they consider to be right and against what they consider to be wrong. Those ways include such diverse phenomena as gossip, ridicule, lynching, terrorism, warfare, feuding, genocide, law, mediation, and avoidance.

a. 1990 Clean Air Act
b. 33 Strategies of War
c. 28-hour day
d. Conflict management

3. In game theory, an _________ is a set of moves or strategies taken by the players, or their payoffs resulting from the actions or strategies taken by all players. The two are complementary in that given knowledge of the set of strategies of all players, the final state of the game is known, as are any relevant payoffs. In a game where chance or a random event is involved, the _________ is not known from only the set of strategies, but is only realized when the random event(s) are realized.

a. A4e
b. A Stake in the Outcome
c. Outcome
d. AAAI

4. The _________ is an international organization designed by its founders to supervise and liberalize international trade. The organization officially commenced on 1 January 1995, under the Marrakesh Agreement, succeeding the 1947 General Agreement on Tariffs and Trade (GATT.)

The _________ deals with regulation of trade between participating countries; it provides a framework for negotiating and formalising trade agreements, and a dispute resolution process aimed at enforcing participants' adherence to _________ agreements which are signed by representatives of member governments and ratified by their parliaments.

a. National Institute for Occupational Safety and Health
b. 1990 Clean Air Act
c. Network planning and design
d. World Trade Organization

5. _________ is one of the managerial functions like planning, organizing, staffing and directing. It is an important function because it helps to check the errors and to take the corrective action so that deviation from standards are minimized and stated goals of the organization are achieved in desired manner.According to modern concepts, _________ is a foreseeing action whereas earlier concept of _________ was used only when errors were detected. _________ in management means setting standards, measuring actual performance and taking corrective action.

a. Control
b. Schedule of reinforcement
c. Decision tree pruning
d. Turnover

6. _________ is a type of thought exhibited by group members who try to minimize conflict and reach consensus without critically testing, analyzing, and evaluating ideas. Individual creativity, uniqueness, and independent thinking are lost in the pursuit of group cohesiveness, as are the advantages of reasonable balance in choice and thought that might normally be obtained by making decisions as a group. During _________, members of the group avoid promoting viewpoints outside the comfort zone of consensus thinking.

a. Self-report inventory
b. Diffusion of responsibility
c. Psychological statistics
d. Groupthink

7. _________ is the pursuit of influencing outcomes -- including public-policy and resource allocation decisions within political, economic, and social systems and institutions -- that directly affect people's current lives. (Cohen, 2001)

Therefore, _________ can be seen as a deliberate process of speaking out on issues of concern in order to exert some influence on behalf of ideas or persons. Based on this definition, Cohen (2001) states that 'ideologues of all persuasions advocate' to bring a change in people's lives.

a. A4e
b. A Stake in the Outcome
c. AAAI
d. Advocacy

8. _________ refers to the process of screening, and selecting qualified people for a job at an organization or firm mid- and large-size organizations and companies often retain professional recruiters or outsource some of the process to _________ agencies. External _________ is the process of attracting and selecting employees from outside the organization.

The _________ industry has four main types of agencies: employment agencies, _________ websites and job search engines, 'headhunters' for executive and professional _________, and in-house _________.

a. Labour hire
b. Referral recruitment
c. Recruitment
d. Recruitment Process Outsourcing

9. In mathematics, a _________ law is (roughly speaking) a formal power series behaving as if it were the product of a Lie group. They were first defined in 1946 by S. Bochner. The term _________ sometimes means the same as _________ law, and sometimes means one of several generalizations.

a. 1990 Clean Air Act
b. 33 Strategies of War
c. 28-hour day
d. Formal group

10. A _________ is a group of employees from various functional areas of the organization - research, engineering, marketing, finance. human resources, and operations, for example - who are all focused on a specific objective and are responsible to work as a team to improve coordination and innovation across divisions and resolve mutual problems.

a. Goal-setting theory
b. Graduate recruitment
c. Sociotechnical systems
d. Cross-functional team

11. _________ refers to the movement of cash into or out of a business or financial product. It is usually measured during a specified, finite period of time. Measurement of _________ can be used

- to determine a project's rate of return or value. The time of _________s into and out of projects are used as inputs in financial models such as internal rate of return, and net present value.
- to determine problems with a business's liquidity. Being profitable does not necessarily mean being liquid. A company can fail because of a shortage of cash, even while profitable.
- as an alternate measure of a business's profits when it is believed that accrual accounting concepts do not represent economic realities. For example, a company may be notionally profitable but generating little operational cash (as may be the case for a company that barters its products rather than selling for cash.) In such a case, the company may be deriving additional operating cash by issuing shares evaluating default risk, re-investment requirements, etc.

_________ is a generic term used differently depending on the context. It may be defined by users for their own purposes.

a. Gross profit margin
b. Gross profit
c. Sweat equity
d. Cash flow

12. A _________ is a volunteer group composed of workers (or even students), usually under the leadership of their supervisor (but they can elect a team leader), who are trained to identify, analyse and solve work-related problems and present their solutions to management in order to improve the performance of the organization, and motivate and enrich the work of employees. When matured, true _________s become self-managing, having gained the confidence of management. _________s are an alternative to the dehumanising concept of the Division of Labour, where workers or individuals are treated like robots.

a. Certified in Production and Inventory Management
b. Competency-based job descriptions
c. Quality circle
d. Connectionist expert systems

13. A _________ -- also known as a geographically dispersed team -- is a group of individuals who work across time, space, and organizational boundaries with links strengthened by webs of communication technology. They have complementary skills and are committed to a common purpose, have interdependent performance goals, and share an approach to work for which they hold themselves mutually accountable. Geographically dispersed teams allow organizations to hire and retain the best people regardless of location.

a. Virtual team
b. Risk management
c. Kanban
d. Trademark

14. A _________ in today's workforce is an individual that is valued for their ability to interpret information within a specific subject area. They will often advance the overall understanding of that subject through focused analysis, design and/or development. They use research skills to define problems and to identify alternatives.

a. Knowledge worker
b. Customer satisfaction
c. Career development
d. Business rule

15. _________ is a term used to classify a group leadership theories that inquire the interactions between leaders and followers. A transactional leader focuses more on a series of 'transactions'. This person is interested in looking out for oneself, having exchange benefits with their subordinates and clarify a sense of duty with rewards and punishments to reach goals.

a. 28-hour day
b. 1990 Clean Air Act
c. Transactional leadership
d. 33 Strategies of War

16. _________ has been described as the 'process of social influence in which one person can enlist the aid and support of others in the accomplishment of a common task' . A definition more inclusive of followers comes from Alan Keith of Genentech who said '_________ is ultimately about creating a way for people to contribute to making something extraordinary happen.'

_________ is one of the most salient aspects of the organizational context. However, defining _________ has been challenging.

a. 28-hour day
b. 1990 Clean Air Act
c. Situational leadership
d. Leadership

17. In the field of human resource management, _________ is the field concerned with organizational activity aimed at bettering the performance of individuals and groups in organizational settings. It has been known by several names, including employee development, human resource development, and learning and development.

Harrison observes that the name was endlessly debated by the Chartered Institute of Personnel and Development during its review of professional standards in 1999/2000.

a. Performance appraisal
b. Training and development
c. Revolving door syndrome
d. Person specification

18. _________ can be regarded as an outcome of mental processes (cognitive process) leading to the selection of a course of action among several alternatives. Every _________ process produces a final choice. The output can be an action or an opinion of choice.

a. 28-hour day
b. 1990 Clean Air Act
c. 33 Strategies of War
d. Decision making

19. _________ is an advertisement in which a particular product specifically mentions a competitor by name for the express purpose of showing why the competitor is inferior to the product naming it.

This should not be confused with parody advertisements, where a fictional product is being advertised for the purpose of poking fun at the particular advertisement, nor should it be confused with the use of a coined brand name for the purpose of comparing the product without actually naming an actual competitor. ('Wikipedia tastes better and is less filling than the Encyclopedia Galactica.')

In the 1980s, during what has been referred to as the cola wars, soft-drink manufacturer Pepsi ran a series of advertisements where people, caught on hidden camera, in a blind taste test, chose Pepsi over rival Coca-Cola.

a. Comparative advertising
b. 28-hour day
c. 1990 Clean Air Act
d. 33 Strategies of War

20. _________ is a concept in ethics with several meanings. It is often used synonymously with such concepts as responsibility, answerability, enforcement, blameworthiness, liability and other terms associated with the expectation of account-giving. As an aspect of governance, it has been central to discussions related to problems in both the public and private (corporation) worlds.

a. Usury
b. Accountability
c. A4e
d. A Stake in the Outcome

21. _________ is individual power based on a high level of identification with, admiration of, or respect for the powerholder.

Nationalism, Patriotism, Celebrities and well-respected people are examples of _________ in effect.

_________ is one of the Five Bases of Social Power, as defined by Bertram Raven and his colleagues[1] in 1959.

a. 33 Strategies of War
b. Referent power
c. 28-hour day
d. 1990 Clean Air Act

22. In the social psychology of groups, _________ is the phenomenon of people making less effort to achieve a goal when they work in a group than when they work alone. This is seen as one of the main reasons groups are sometimes less productive than the combined performance of their members working as individuals.

- Ringelmann, Max : 1913

Research began in 1913 with Max Ringelmann's study. He found that when he asked a group of men to pull on a rope, that they did not pull as hard, or put as much effort into the activity, as they did when they were pulling alone.

a. Machiavellianism
b. Social loafing
c. Personal space
d. Self-enhancement

23. _________ is a civil designation for persons who are incorporated in a fixed or permanent way to a society or group: regular member of the working staff, permanent staff distinguished from a supernumerary.

The term '_________' and its counterpart, 'supernumerary,' originated in Spanish and Latin American academy and government; it is now also used in countries all over the world, such as France, the U.S., England, Italy, etc.

There are _________ members of surgical organizations, of universities, of gastronomical associations, etc.

a. Numerary
b. Abraham Harold Maslow
c. Affiliation
d. Adam Smith

24. The _________ is the Cabinet department of the United States government concerned with promoting economic growth. It was originally created as the _________ and Labor on February 14, 1903. It was subsequently renamed to the Department of Commerce on March 4, 1913, and its bureaus and agencies specializing in labor were transferred to the new Department of Labor.

a. A Stake in the Outcome
b. AAAI
c. United States Department of Commerce
d. A4e

25. _________ is subcontracting a process, such as product design or manufacturing, to a third-party company. The decision to outsource is often made in the interest of lowering cost or making better use of time and energy costs, redirecting or conserving energy directed at the competencies of a particular business, or to make more efficient use of land, labor, capital, (information) technology and resources. _________ became part of the business lexicon during the 1980s.

a. Operant conditioning
b. Opinion leadership
c. Outsourcing
d. Unemployment insurance

26. _________ is a technique of planning and decision-making which reverses the working process of traditional budgeting. In traditional incremental budgeting, departmental managers justify only increases over the previous year budget and what has been already spent is automatically sanctioned. No reference is made to the previous level of expenditure.

a. 1990 Clean Air Act
b. 28-hour day
c. 33 Strategies of War
d. Zero-based budgeting

27. _________ in its literal sense is the process of transformation of local or regional phenomena into global ones. It can be described as a process by which the people of the world are unified into a single society and function together.

This process is a combination of economic, technological, sociocultural and political forces.

a. Collaborative Planning, Forecasting and Replenishment
b. Cost Management
c. Histogram
d. Globalization

28. The term _________ in logic applies to arguments or statements.

An argument is valid if and only if the truth of its premises entails the truth of its conclusion, it would be self-contradictory to affirm the premises and deny the conclusion. The corresponding conditional of a valid argument is a logical truth and the negation of its corresponding conditional is a contradiction.

a. Fuzzy logic
b. 1990 Clean Air Act
c. Simplification
d. Validity

1. _________ has been described as the 'process of social influence in which one person can enlist the aid and support of others in the accomplishment of a common task' . A definition more inclusive of followers comes from Alan Keith of Genentech who said '_________ is ultimately about creating a way for people to contribute to making something extraordinary happen.'

_________ is one of the most salient aspects of the organizational context. However, defining _________ has been challenging.

a. 1990 Clean Air Act
b. Situational leadership
c. 28-hour day
d. Leadership

2. The _________ (Situation, Task, Action, Result) format is a job interview technique used by interviewers to gather all the relevant information about a specific capability that the job requires. This interview format is said to have a higher degree of predictability of future on-the-job performance than the traditional interview.

- Situation: The interviewer wants you to present a recent challenge and situation in which you found yourself.
- Task: What did you have to achieve? The interviewer will be looking to see what you were trying to achieve from the situation.
- Action: What did you do? The interviewer will be looking for information on what you did, why you did it and what were the alternatives.
- Results: What was the outcome of your actions? What did you achieve through your actions and did you meet your objectives. What did you learn from this experience and have you used this learning since?

.

a. Rasch models
b. Phrase completion
c. Competency-based job descriptions
d. Star

3. _________ is a process of agreeing upon objectives within an organization so that management and employees agree to the objectives and understand what they are in the organization.

The term '_________' was first popularized by Peter Drucker in his 1954 book 'The Practice of Management'.

The essence of _________ is participative goal setting, choosing course of actions and decision making.

a. Job enrichment
b. Clean sheet review
c. Business economics
d. Management by objectives

4. _________ is an idea in the field of Organizational studies and management which describes the psychology, attitudes, experiences, beliefs and Values (personal and cultural values) of an organization. It has been defined as 'the specific collection of values and norms that are shared by people and groups in an organization and that control the way they interact with each other and with stakeholders outside the organization.'

This definition continues to explain organizational values also known as 'beliefs and ideas about what kinds of goals members of an organization should pursue and ideas about the appropriate kinds or standards of behavior organizational members should use to achieve these goals. From organizational values develop organizational norms, guidelines or expectations that prescribe appropriate kinds of behavior by employees in particular situations and control the behavior of organizational members towards one another.'

_________ is not the same as corporate culture.

a. Organizational effectiveness
b. Organizational development
c. Union shop
d. Organizational culture

5. _________ is individual power based on a high level of identification with, admiration of, or respect for the powerholder.

Nationalism, Patriotism, Celebrities and well-respected people are examples of _________ in effect.

_________ is one of the Five Bases of Social Power, as defined by Bertram Raven and his colleagues[1] in 1959.

a. Referent power
b. 1990 Clean Air Act
c. 33 Strategies of War
d. 28-hour day

6. A _________ is an alliance among individuals or groups, during which they cooperate in joint action, each in his own self-interest, joining forces together for a common cause. This alliance may be temporary or a matter of convenience. A _________ thus differs from a more formal covenant.

a. Coalition
b. 1990 Clean Air Act
c. 33 Strategies of War
d. 28-hour day

7. _________ is a form of social influence. It is the process of guiding people and oneself toward the adoption of an idea, attitude, or action by rational and symbolic (though not always logical) means. It is strategy of problem-solving relying on 'appeals' rather than coercion.

a. Social loafing
b. Persuasion
c. Self-enhancement
d. Personal space

8. _________ , often measured as an _________ Quotient (EQ), is a term that describes the ability, capacity, skill or (in the case of the trait _________ model) a self-perceived ability, to identify, assess, and manage the emotions of one's self, of others, and of groups. Different models have been proposed for the definition of _________ and disagreement exists as to how the term should be used. Despite these disagreements, which are often highly technical, the ability _________ and trait _________ models (but not the mixed models) are enjoying considerable support in the literature and have successful applications in many different domains.

a. AAAI
b. Emotional Intelligence
c. A4e
d. A Stake in the Outcome

9. Social consciousness is consciousness shared within a society. It can also be defined as _________; to be aware of the problems that different societies and communities face on a day-to-day basis; to be conscious of the difficulties and hardships of society.

There is debate as to exactly what the term means.

a. Soft skill
b. Self-disclosure
c. Role conflict
d. Social awareness

10. The trait of _________ is a central dimension of human personality. Extraverts (also spelled extroverts) tend to be gregarious, assertive, and interested in seeking out excitement. Introverts, in contrast, tend to be more reserved, less outgoing, and less sociable.

a. A4e
b. A Stake in the Outcome
c. AAAI
d. Extraversion-introversion

11. _________ is the act by an employer of terminating employment. Though such a decision can be made by an employer for a variety of reasons, ranging from an economic downturn to performance-related problems on the part of the employee, being fired has a strong stigma in many cultures. To be fired, as opposed to quitting voluntarily (or being laid off), is often perceived as being the employee's fault, and is therefore considered to be disgraceful and a sign of failure.

a. Termination of employment
b. Firing
c. Severance package
d. Layoff

12. _________ is one of five major domains of personality discovered by psychologists. Openness involves active imagination, aesthetic sensitivity, attentiveness to inner feelings, preference for variety, and intellectual curiosity. A great deal of psychometric research has demonstrated that these qualities are statistically correlated.

a. Openness to experience
b. Introversion
c. Extraversion
d. Introverts

13. _________ is a term defined by the Oxford English Dictionary as an individual's 'course or progress through life '. It is usually considered to pertain to remunerative work (and sometimes also formal education.)

The etymology of the term is somewhat ironic in that it comes from the Latin word carrera, which means race .

a. Career planning
b. Career
c. Spatial mismatch
d. Nursing shortage

14. The _________ captures an expanded spectrum of values and criteria for measuring organizational success: economic, ecological and social. With the ratification of the United Nations and ICLEI _________ standard for urban and community accounting in early 2007, this became the dominant approach to public sector full cost accounting. Similar UN standards apply to natural capital and human capital measurement to assist in measurements required by _________, e.g. the ecoBudget standard for reporting ecological footprint.

a. Triple bottom line
b. 33 Strategies of War
c. 1990 Clean Air Act
d. 28-hour day

15. _________ in its literal sense is the process of transformation of local or regional phenomena into global ones. It can be described as a process by which the people of the world are unified into a single society and function together.

This process is a combination of economic, technological, sociocultural and political forces.

a. Collaborative Planning, Forecasting and Replenishment
b. Cost Management
c. Globalization
d. Histogram

16. _________ is the strategic and coherent approach to the management of an organisation's most valued assets - the people working there who individually and collectively contribute to the achievement of the objectives of the business. The terms '_________' and 'human resources' (HR) have largely replaced the term 'personnel management' as a description of the processes involved in managing people in organizations. In simple sense, _________ means employing people, developing their resources, utilizing, maintaining and compensating their services in tune with the job and organizational requirement.

a. Progressive discipline
b. Job knowledge
c. Human resource management
d. Revolving door syndrome

17. _________ can be regarded as an outcome of mental processes (cognitive process) leading to the selection of a course of action among several alternatives. Every _________ process produces a final choice. The output can be an action or an opinion of choice.

a. 28-hour day
b. Decision Making
c. 1990 Clean Air Act
d. 33 Strategies of War

18. The term _________ refers to a salaried professional or an educated worker who performs semi-professional office, administrative, and sales coordination tasks, as opposed to a blue-collar worker, whose job requires manual labor. 'White-collar work' is an informal term, defined in contrast to 'blue-collar work'.

The term 'white collar' was first used by Upton Sinclair in relation to modern clerical, administrative and management workers during the 1930s.

a. 28-hour day
b. 33 Strategies of War
c. 1990 Clean Air Act
d. White-collar worker

19. A _________ is a member of the working class who typically performs manual labor and earns an hourly wage. _________s are distinguished from those in the service sector and from white-collar workers, whose jobs are not considered manual labor.

Blue-collar work may be skilled or unskilled, and may involve manufacturing, mining, building and construction trades, mechanical work, maintenance, repair and operations maintenance or technical installations.

a. 1990 Clean Air Act
b. 33 Strategies of War
c. 28-hour day
d. Blue-collar worker

20. _________ refers to techniques, processes and tools for organizing and coordinating a group of individuals working towards a common goal--i.e. a team.

Several well-known approaches to _________ have come out of academic work. Examples include the Belbin Team Inventory by Meredith Belbin, a method to identify the different types of personalities within teams, and Ken Blanchard's description of 'High Performing Teams'.

a. 28-hour day
b. 1990 Clean Air Act
c. 33 Strategies of War
d. Team management

21. _________ is a 'policy by which management devotes its time to investigating only those situations in which actual results differ significantly from planned results. The idea is that management should spend its valuable time concentrating on the more important items (such as shaping the company's future strategic course.) Attention is given only to material deviations requiring investigation.'

It is not entirely synonymous with the concept of exception management in that it describes a policy where absolute focus is on exception management, in contrast to moderate application of exception management.

a. Trustee
b. Management by exception
c. C-A-K-E
d. Business philosophy

22. _________ is one of the managerial functions like planning, organizing, staffing and directing. It is an important function because it helps to check the errors and to take the corrective action so that deviation from standards are minimized and stated goals of the organization are achieved in desired manner.According to modern concepts, _________ is a foreseeing action whereas earlier concept of _________ was used only when errors were detected. _________ in management means setting standards, measuring actual performance and taking corrective action.

a. Turnover
b. Decision tree pruning
c. Schedule of reinforcement
d. Control

23. A _________ -- also known as a geographically dispersed team -- is a group of individuals who work across time, space, and organizational boundaries with links strengthened by webs of communication technology. They have complementary skills and are committed to a common purpose, have interdependent performance goals, and share an approach to work for which they hold themselves mutually accountable. Geographically dispersed teams allow organizations to hire and retain the best people regardless of location.

a. Trademark
b. Virtual team
c. Risk management
d. Kanban

24. The _________ refers to a cognitive bias whereby the perception of a particular trait is influenced by the perception of the former traits in a sequence of interpretations.

Edward L. Thorndike was the first to support the _________ with empirical research. In a psychology study published in 1920, Thorndike asked commanding officers to rate their soldiers; Thorndike found high cross-correlation between all positive and all negative traits.

a. Sunk costs
b. Distinction bias
c. Cognitive biases
d. Halo effect

25. _________ for short is a descriptive term for certain executives in a business operation. It is also a formal title held by some business executives, most commonly in the hospitality industry.

A _________ has broad, overall responsibility for a business or organization. Whereas a manager may be responsible for one functional area, the _________ is responsible for all areas.

a. General manager
b. Chief technology officer
c. Chief knowledge officer
d. Managing director

26. Contingency leadership theory in organizational studies is a type of leadership theory, leadership style, and leadership model that presumes that different leadership styles are contingent to different situations. It is also referred as _________ Â® theory although, as originally convened, the situational theory term is much more restrictive. The original situational theory argues that the best type of leadership is totally determined by the situational variables.Currently there are many styles of leadership.

a. Situational theory
b. 28-hour day
c. 1990 Clean Air Act
d. Situational leadership

27. _________ is a term used to classify a group leadership theories that inquire the interactions between leaders and followers. A transactional leader focuses more on a series of 'transactions'. This person is interested in looking out for oneself, having exchange benefits with their subordinates and clarify a sense of duty with rewards and punishments to reach goals.

a. 33 Strategies of War
b. Transactional leadership
c. 1990 Clean Air Act
d. 28-hour day

28. _________ is a leadership style that defines as leadership that creates voluble and positive change in the followers. A transformational leader focuses on 'transforming' others to help each other, to look out for each other, be encouraging, harmonious, and look out for the organization as a whole. In this leadership, the leader enhances the motivation, moral and performance of his follower group.

a. SESAMO
b. Transformational leadership
c. Polynomial conjoint measurement
d. Strong-Campbell Interest Inventory

29. The act of becoming a surety is also called a _________. Traditionally a _________ was distinguished from a surety in that the surety's liability was joint and primary with the principal, whereas the guaranty's liability was ancillary and derivative, but many jurisdictions have abolished this distinction

a. Clayton Antitrust Act
b. Guarantee
c. National treatment
d. Blue sky law

30. _________, e-commuting, e-work, telework, working from home (WFH), or working at home (WAH) is a work arrangement in which employees enjoy flexibility in working location and hours. In other words, the daily commute to a central place of work is replaced by telecommunication links. Many work from home, while others, occasionally also referred to as nomad workers or web commuters utilize mobile telecommunications technology to work from coffee shops or myriad other locations.

a. 28-hour day
b. 33 Strategies of War
c. 1990 Clean Air Act
d. Telecommuting

31. _________ is a term in psychology which refers to a person's belief about what causes the good or bad results in his or her life, either in general or in a specific area such as health or academics. Understanding of the concept was developed by Julian B. Rotter in 1954, and has since become an important aspect of personality studies.

_________ refers to the extent to which individuals believe that they can control events that affect them.

a. Self-enhancement
b. Machiavellianism
c. Social loafing
d. Locus of control

32. _________ is a process of planning and controlling the performance or execution of any type of activity, such as:

- a project (project _________) or
- a process (process _________, sometimes referred to as the process performance measurement and management system.)

Organization's senior management is responsible for carrying out its _________.

a. Management process
b. Participatory management
c. Work design
d. Human Relations Movement

33. _________ is the temporary suspension or permanent termination of employment of an employee or (more commonly) a group of employees for business reasons, such as the decision that certain positions are no longer necessary or a business slow-down or interruption in work. Originally the term '_________' referred exclusively to a temporary interruption in work, as when factory work cyclically falls off. However, in recent times the term can also refer to the permanent elimination of a position.

a. Retirement
b. Layoff
c. Termination of employment
d. Wrongful dismissal

1. _________ refers to the long-term management of intractable conflicts. It is the label for the variety of ways by which people handle grievances--standing up for what they consider to be right and against what they consider to be wrong. Those ways include such diverse phenomena as gossip, ridicule, lynching, terrorism, warfare, feuding, genocide, law, mediation, and avoidance.

a. 28-hour day
b. Conflict management
c. 1990 Clean Air Act
d. 33 Strategies of War

2. _________ is a broad label that refers to any individuals or households that use goods and services generated within the economy. The concept of a _________ is used in different contexts, so that the usage and significance of the term may vary.

Typically when business people and economists talk of _________s they are talking about person as _________, an aggregated commodity item with little individuality other than that expressed in the buy/not-buy decision.

a. 33 Strategies of War
b. 28-hour day
c. 1990 Clean Air Act
d. Consumer

3. _________ is one of the managerial functions like planning, organizing, staffing and directing. It is an important function because it helps to check the errors and to take the corrective action so that deviation from standards are minimized and stated goals of the organization are achieved in desired manner.According to modern concepts, _________ is a foreseeing action whereas earlier concept of _________ was used only when errors were detected. _________ in management means setting standards, measuring actual performance and taking corrective action.

a. Decision tree pruning
b. Control
c. Schedule of reinforcement
d. Turnover

4. _________ describes the situation when output from (or information about the result of) an event or phenomenon in the past will influence the same event/phenomenon in the present or future. When an event is part of a chain of cause-and-effect that forms a circuit or loop, then the event is said to 'feed back' into itself.

_________ is also a synonym for:

- _________ signal; the information about the initial event that is the basis for subsequent modification of the event.
- _________ loop; the causal path that leads from the initial generation of the _________ signal to the subsequent modification of the event.

_________ is a mechanism, process or signal that is looped back to control a system within itself. Such a loop is called a _________ loop.

a. Positive feedback
b. 1990 Clean Air Act
c. Feedback loop
d. Feedback

5. _________ is a field of study that looks at how people from differing cultural backgrounds endeavour to communicate.

In years during and preceding the Cold War, the United States economy was largely self-contained because the world was polarized into two separate and competing powers: the east and west. However, changes and advancements in economic relationships, political systems, and technological options began to break down old cultural barriers.

a. 28-hour day
b. Cross-cultural communication
c. 1990 Clean Air Act
d. 33 Strategies of War

6. The term _________ refers to a salaried professional or an educated worker who performs semi-professional office, administrative, and sales coordination tasks, as opposed to a blue-collar worker, whose job requires manual labor. 'White-collar work' is an informal term, defined in contrast to 'blue-collar work'.

The term 'white collar' was first used by Upton Sinclair in relation to modern clerical, administrative and management workers during the 1930s.

a. 1990 Clean Air Act
b. 33 Strategies of War
c. 28-hour day
d. White-collar worker

7. _________ is an effective method of monitoring a process through the use of control charts. Control charts enable the use of objective criteria for distinguishing background variation from events of significance based on statistical techniques. Much of its power lies in the ability to monitor both process center and its variation about that center.

a. Statistical process control
b. Process capability
c. Single Minute Exchange of Die
d. Quality control

8. _________ is a contract between two parties, one being the employer and the other being the employee. An employee may be defined as: 'A person in the service of another under any contract of hire, express or implied, oral or written, where the employer has the power or right to control and direct the employee in the material details of how the work is to be performed.' Black's Law Dictionary page 471 (5th ed. 1979.)

a. Employment
b. Exit interview
c. Employment counsellor
d. Employment rate

9. The term _________ was created by President Lyndon B. Johnson when he signed Executive Order 11246 on September 24, 1965, created to prohibit federal contractors from discriminating against employees on the basis of race, sex, creed, religion, color, or national origin. In more recent times, most employers have also added sexual orientation to the list of non-discrimination.

The Executive Order also required contractors to implement affirmative action plans to increase the participation of minorities and women in the workplace.

a. A Stake in the Outcome
b. Equal Employment Opportunity
c. AAAI
d. A4e

10. The act of becoming a surety is also called a _________. Traditionally a _________ was distinguished from a surety in that the surety's liability was joint and primary with the principal, whereas the guaranty's liability was ancillary and derivative, but many jurisdictions have abolished this distinction

a. Blue sky law
b. National treatment
c. Guarantee
d. Clayton Antitrust Act

11. An _________ is a private network that uses Internet protocols, network connectivity, and possibly the public telecommunication system to securely share part of an organization's information or operations with suppliers, vendors, partners, customers or other businesses. An _________ can be viewed as part of a company's intranet that is extended to users outside the company (e.g.: normally over the Internet.) It has also been described as a 'state of mind' in which the Internet is perceived as a way to do business with a preapproved set of other companies business-to-business (B2B), in isolation from all other Internet users.

a. AAAI
b. A Stake in the Outcome
c. A4e
d. Extranet

12. An _________ is a private computer network that uses Internet technologies to securely share any part of an organization's information or operational systems with its employees. Sometimes the term refers only to the organization's internal website, but often it is a more extensive part of the organization's computer infrastructure and private websites are an important component and focal point of internal communication and collaboration.

An _________ is built from the same concepts and technologies used for the Internet, such as client-server computing and the Internet Protocol Suite (TCP/IP.)

a. A4e
b. AAAI
c. A Stake in the Outcome
d. Intranet

13. _________ is a Japanese philosophy that focuses on continuous improvement throughout all aspects of life. When applied to the workplace, _________ activities continually improve all functions of a business, from manufacturing to management and from the CEO to the assembly line workers. By improving standardized activities and processes, _________ aims to eliminate waste .

a. Psychological pricing
b. Sensitivity analysis
c. Kaizen
d. Cross-docking

14. _________, e-commuting, e-work, telework, working from home (WFH), or working at home (WAH) is a work arrangement in which employees enjoy flexibility in working location and hours. In other words, the daily commute to a central place of work is replaced by telecommunication links. Many work from home, while others, occasionally also referred to as nomad workers or web commuters utilize mobile telecommunications technology to work from coffee shops or myriad other locations.

a. 28-hour day
b. 33 Strategies of War
c. Telecommuting
d. 1990 Clean Air Act

15. _________ comprises a range of practices used in an organisation to identify, create, represent, distribute and enable adoption of insights and experiences. Such insights and experiences comprise knowledge, either embodied in individuals or embedded in organisational processes or practice.

An established discipline since 1991 , _________ includes courses taught in the fields of business administration, information systems, management, and library and information sciences .

a. 28-hour day
b. 1990 Clean Air Act
c. 33 Strategies of War
d. Knowledge management

16. The 'business case for _________', theorizes that in a global marketplace, a company that employs a diverse workforce (both men and women, people of many generations, people from ethnically and racially diverse backgrounds etc.) is better able to understand the demographics of the marketplace it serves and is thus better equipped to thrive in that marketplace than a company that has a more limited range of employee demographics.

An additional corollary suggests that a company that supports the _________ of its workforce can also improve employee satisfaction, productivity and retention.

a. Virtual team
b. Diversity
c. Trademark
d. Kanban

17. A _________ is an entity formed between two or more parties to undertake economic activity together. The parties agree to create a new entity by both contributing equity, and they then share in the revenues, expenses, and control of the enterprise. The venture can be for one specific project only, or a continuing business relationship such as the Fuji Xerox _________.

a. Joint venture
b. Meritor Savings Bank v. Vinson
c. Civil Rights Act of 1991
d. Patent

18. An _________ is a person who has possession of an enterprise and assumes significant accountability for the inherent risks and the outcome. It is an ambitious leader who combines land, labor, and capital to create and market new goods or services. The term is a loanword from French and was first defined by the Irish economist Richard Cantillon.

a. A Stake in the Outcome
b. AAAI
c. A4e
d. Entrepreneur

19. _________ are, simply put, various approaches or ways of learning. They involve educating methods, particular to an individual, that are presumed to allow that individual to learn best. It is commonly believed that most people favor some particular method of interacting with, taking in, and processing stimuli or information.

a. Learning styles
b. 28-hour day
c. 33 Strategies of War
d. 1990 Clean Air Act

20. _________ according to Onuoha (2007) is the practice of starting new organizations or revitalizing mature organizations, particularly new businesses generally in response to identified opportunities. _________ is often a difficult undertaking, as a vast majority of new businesses fail. Entrepreneurial activities are substantially different depending on the type of organization that is being started.

a. A4e
b. AAAI
c. A Stake in the Outcome
d. Entrepreneurship

21. In a military context, the _________ is the line of authority and responsibility along which orders are passed within a military unit and between different units. The term is also used in a civilian management context describing comparable hierarchical structures of authority.

a. 1990 Clean Air Act
b. 28-hour day
c. French leave
d. Chain of command

22. _________ is the branch of economics that studies the dynamics of exchange rates, foreign investment, and how these affect international trade. It also studies international projects, international investments and capital flows, and trade deficits. It includes the study of futures, options and currency swaps.

a. AAAI
b. A4e
c. A Stake in the Outcome
d. International finance

23. An _________ is a situation that will often involve an apparent conflict between moral imperatives, in which to obey one would result in transgressing another. This is also called an ethical paradox since in moral philosophy, paradox plays a central role in ethics debates. For instance, an ethical admonition to 'love thy neighbour as thy self' is not always just in contrast with, but sometimes in contradiction to an armed neighbour actively trying to kill you: if he or she succeeds, you will not be able to love him or her.

a. Ethical dilemma
b. A4e
c. A Stake in the Outcome
d. AAAI

24. _________ has been described as the 'process of social influence in which one person can enlist the aid and support of others in the accomplishment of a common task' . A definition more inclusive of followers comes from Alan Keith of Genentech who said '_________ is ultimately about creating a way for people to contribute to making something extraordinary happen.'

_________ is one of the most salient aspects of the organizational context. However, defining _________ has been challenging.

a. 1990 Clean Air Act
b. 28-hour day
c. Situational leadership
d. Leadership

1. _________ is one of the managerial functions like planning, organizing, staffing and directing. It is an important function because it helps to check the errors and to take the corrective action so that deviation from standards are minimized and stated goals of the organization are achieved in desired manner.According to modern concepts, _________ is a foreseeing action whereas earlier concept of _________ was used only when errors were detected. _________ in management means setting standards, measuring actual performance and taking corrective action.

a. Decision tree pruning
b. Turnover
c. Schedule of reinforcement
d. Control

2. The 'business case for _________', theorizes that in a global marketplace, a company that employs a diverse workforce (both men and women, people of many generations, people from ethnically and racially diverse backgrounds etc.) is better able to understand the demographics of the marketplace it serves and is thus better equipped to thrive in that marketplace than a company that has a more limited range of employee demographics.

An additional corollary suggests that a company that supports the _________ of its workforce can also improve employee satisfaction, productivity and retention.

a. Diversity
b. Trademark
c. Kanban
d. Virtual team

3. _________ refers to the process of screening, and selecting qualified people for a job at an organization or firm mid- and large-size organizations and companies often retain professional recruiters or outsource some of the process to _________ agencies. External _________ is the process of attracting and selecting employees from outside the organization.

The _________ industry has four main types of agencies: employment agencies, _________ websites and job search engines, 'headhunters' for executive and professional _________, and in-house _________.

a. Labour hire
b. Referral recruitment
c. Recruitment Process Outsourcing
d. Recruitment

4. _________ refers to metrics and measures of output from production processes, per unit of input. Labor _________, for example, is typically measured as a ratio of output per labor-hour, an input. _________ may be conceived of as a metrics of the technical or engineering efficiency of production.

a. Productivity
b. Master production schedule
c. Value engineering
d. Remanufacturing

5. In economics, _________ is the desire to own something and the ability to pay for it. The term _________ signifies the ability or the willingness to buy a particular commodity at a given point of time.

a. 28-hour day
b. 33 Strategies of War
c. 1990 Clean Air Act
d. Demand

6. _________ is a work methodology based on the parallelization of tasks (ie. concurrently.) It refers to an approach used in product development in which functions of design engineering, manufacturing engineering and other functions are integrated to reduce the elapsed time required to bring a new product to the market.

a. Critical Chain Project Management
b. Concurrent engineering
c. Project management
d. Work package

7. '_________ is a conflict among the roles corresponding to two or more statuses.'

_________ is a special form of social conflict that takes place when one is forced to take on two different and incompatible roles at the same time. Consider the example of a doctor who is himself a patient, or who must decide whether he should be present for his daughter's birthday party (in his role as 'father') or attend an ailing patient (as 'doctor'.) (Also compare the psychological concept of cognitive dissonance.)

a. Role conflict
b. Self-disclosure
c. Social network analysis
d. Soft skill

8. _________ is a 'policy by which management devotes its time to investigating only those situations in which actual results differ significantly from planned results. The idea is that management should spend its valuable time concentrating on the more important items (such as shaping the company's future strategic course.) Attention is given only to material deviations requiring investigation.'

It is not entirely synonymous with the concept of exception management in that it describes a policy where absolute focus is on exception management, in contrast to moderate application of exception management.

a. Management by exception
b. C-A-K-E
c. Trustee
d. Business philosophy

9. _________ refers to the long-term management of intractable conflicts. It is the label for the variety of ways by which people handle grievances--standing up for what they consider to be right and against what they consider to be wrong. Those ways include such diverse phenomena as gossip, ridicule, lynching, terrorism, warfare, feuding, genocide, law, mediation, and avoidance.

a. 28-hour day
b. 33 Strategies of War
c. 1990 Clean Air Act
d. Conflict management

10. _________ describes the situation when output from (or information about the result of) an event or phenomenon in the past will influence the same event/phenomenon in the present or future. When an event is part of a chain of cause-and-effect that forms a circuit or loop, then the event is said to 'feed back' into itself.

_________ is also a synonym for:

- _________ signal; the information about the initial event that is the basis for subsequent modification of the event.
- _________ loop; the causal path that leads from the initial generation of the _________ signal to the subsequent modification of the event.

_________ is a mechanism, process or signal that is looped back to control a system within itself. Such a loop is called a _________ loop.

a. 1990 Clean Air Act
b. Feedback loop
c. Positive feedback
d. Feedback

11. _________ is an increasingly broadening term with which an organization, or other human system describes the combination of traditionally administrative personnel functions with acquisition and application of skills, knowledge and experience, Employee Relations and resource planning at various levels. The field draws upon concepts developed in Industrial/Organizational Psychology and System Theory. _________ has at least two related interpretations depending on context. The original usage derives from political economy and economics, where it was traditionally called labor, one of four factors of production although this perspective is changing as a function of new and ongoing research into more strategic approaches at national levels. This first usage is used more in terms of '_________ development', and can go beyond just organizations to the level of nations . The more traditional usage within corporations and businesses refers to the individuals within a firm or agency, and to the portion of the organization that deals with hiring, firing, training, and other personnel issues, typically referred to as `_________ management'.

a. Progressive discipline
b. Human resources
c. Human resource management
d. Bradford Factor

12. _________ generally refers to a list of all planned expenses and revenues. It is a plan for saving and spending. A _________ is an important concept in microeconomics, which uses a _________ line to illustrate the trade-offs between two or more goods.

a. 33 Strategies of War
b. 28-hour day
c. 1990 Clean Air Act
d. Budget

13. _________ is a technique of planning and decision-making which reverses the working process of traditional budgeting. In traditional incremental budgeting, departmental managers justify only increases over the previous year budget and what has been already spent is automatically sanctioned. No reference is made to the previous level of expenditure.

a. 1990 Clean Air Act
b. 33 Strategies of War
c. 28-hour day
d. Zero-based budgeting

14. In business and accounting, _________s are everything of value that is owned by a person or company. Any property or object of value that one possesses, usually considered as applicable to the payment of one's debts is considered an _________. Simplistically stated, _________s are things of value that can be readily converted into cash.

a. AAAI
b. Asset
c. A Stake in the Outcome
d. A4e

15. The general definition of an _________ is an evaluation of a person, organization, system, process, project or product. _________s are performed to ascertain the validity and reliability of information; also to provide an assessment of a system's internal control. The goal of an _________ is to express an opinion on the person / organization/system (etc) in question, under evaluation based on work done on a test basis.

a. Audit
b. Internal control
c. A Stake in the Outcome
d. Audit committee

16. In financial accounting, a _________ or statement of financial position is a summary of a person's or organization's balances. Assets, liabilities and ownership equity are listed as of a specific date, such as the end of its financial year. A _________ is often described as a snapshot of a company's financial condition.

a. Balance sheet
b. 33 Strategies of War
c. 1990 Clean Air Act
d. 28-hour day

17. In accounting, a _________ is an asset on the balance sheet which is expected to be sold or otherwise used up in the near future, usually within one year, or one business cycle - whichever is longer. Typical _________s include cash, cash equivalents, accounts receivable, inventory, the portion of prepaid accounts which will be used within a year, and short-term investments.

On the balance sheet, assets will typically be classified into _________s and long-term assets.

a. Matching principle
b. Treasury stock
c. Net income
d. Current asset

18. _________ are formal records of the financial activities of a business, person, or other entity. In British English, including United Kingdom company law, _________ are often referred to as accounts, although the term _________ is also used, particularly by accountants.

_________ provide an overview of a business or person's financial condition in both short and long term.

a. 1990 Clean Air Act
b. Financial statements
c. 33 Strategies of War
d. 28-hour day

19. _________ plant, and equipment, is a term used in accountancy for assets and property which cannot easily be converted into cash. This can be compared with current assets such as cash or bank accounts, which are described as liquid assets. In most cases, only tangible assets are referred to as fixed.

a. 33 Strategies of War
b. Fixed asset
c. 1990 Clean Air Act
d. 28-hour day

20. _________ is a company's financial statement that indicates how the revenue is transformed into the net income The purpose of the _________ is to show managers and investors whether the company made or lost money during the period being reported.

The important thing to remember about an _________ is that it represents a period of time.

a. AAAI
b. A Stake in the Outcome
c. A4e
d. Income statement

21. Market _________ is a business, economics or investment term that refers to an asset's ability to be easily converted through an act of buying or selling without causing a significant movement in the price and with minimum loss of value. Money, or cash on hand, is the most liquid asset. An act of exchange of a less liquid asset with a more liquid asset is called liquidation.

a. 28-hour day
b. 1990 Clean Air Act
c. 33 Strategies of War
d. Liquidity

22. An _________ is a practitioner of accountancy, which is the measurement, disclosure or provision of assurance about financial information that helps managers, investors, tax authorities and other decision makers make resource allocation decisions.

The word '_________' is derived from the French 'Compter' which took its origin from the Latin 'Computare'. The word was formerly written in English as 'Accomptant', but in process of time the word, which was always pronounced by dropping the 'p', became gradually changed both in pronunciation and in orthography to its present form.

a. A Stake in the Outcome
b. Accountant
c. A4e
d. AAAI

23. The _________ captures an expanded spectrum of values and criteria for measuring organizational success: economic, ecological and social. With the ratification of the United Nations and ICLEI _________ standard for urban and community accounting in early 2007, this became the dominant approach to public sector full cost accounting. Similar UN standards apply to natural capital and human capital measurement to assist in measurements required by _________, e.g. the ecoBudget standard for reporting ecological footprint.

a. Triple bottom line
b. 28-hour day
c. 1990 Clean Air Act
d. 33 Strategies of War

24. _________ is a business management strategy aimed at embedding awareness of quality in all organizational processes. _________ has been widely used in manufacturing, education, hospitals, call centers, government, and service industries, as well as NASA space and science programs.

As defined by the International Organization for Standardization (ISO):

> '_________ is a management approach for an organization, centered on quality, based on the participation of all its members and aiming at long-term success through customer satisfaction, and benefits to all members of the organization and to society.' ISO 8402:1994

One major aim is to reduce variation from every process so that greater consistency of effort is obtained. (Royse, D., Thyer, B., Padgett D., ' Logan T., 2006)

a. Total quality management
b. 1990 Clean Air Act
c. 28-hour day
d. Quality management

25. _________ refers to techniques, processes and tools for organizing and coordinating a group of individuals working towards a common goal--i.e. a team.

Several well-known approaches to _________ have come out of academic work. Examples include the Belbin Team Inventory by Meredith Belbin, a method to identify the different types of personalities within teams, and Ken Blanchard's description of 'High Performing Teams'.

a. Team management
b. 1990 Clean Air Act
c. 33 Strategies of War
d. 28-hour day

26. _________ can be considered to have three main components: quality control, quality assurance and quality improvement. _________ is focused not only on product quality, but also the means to achieve it. _________ therefore uses quality assurance and control of processes as well as products to achieve more consistent quality.

a. Quality management
b. 28-hour day
c. Total quality management
d. 1990 Clean Air Act

27. In probability theory, a probability distribution is called _________ if its cumulative distribution function is _________. This is equivalent to saying that for random variables X with the distribution in question, Pr[X = a] = 0 for all real numbers a, i.e.: the probability that X attains the value a is zero, for any number a. If the distribution of X is _________ then X is called a _________ random variable.

a. Connectionist expert systems
b. Continuous
c. Decision tree pruning
d. Pay Band

28. _________ is a management process whereby delivery (customer valued) processes are constantly evaluated and improved in the light of their efficiency, effectiveness and flexibility.

Some see it as a meta process for most management systems (Business Process Management, Quality Management, Project Management). Deming saw it as part of the 'system' whereby feedback from the process and customer were evaluated against organisational goals.

a. Sole proprietorship
b. First-mover advantage
c. Critical Success Factor
d. Continuous Improvement Process

29. _________ is the process of comparing the cost, cycle time, productivity, or quality of a specific process or method to another that is widely considered to be an industry standard or best practice. Essentially, _________ provides a snapshot of the performance of your business and helps you understand where you are in relation to a particular standard. The result is often a business case for making changes in order to make improvements.

a. Complementors
b. Competitive heterogeneity
c. Benchmarking
d. Cost leadership

30. A _________ is a volunteer group composed of workers (or even students), usually under the leadership of their supervisor (but they can elect a team leader), who are trained to identify, analyse and solve work-related problems and present their solutions to management in order to improve the performance of the organization, and motivate and enrich the work of employees. When matured, true _________s become self-managing, having gained the confidence of management. _________s are an alternative to the dehumanising concept of the Division of Labour, where workers or individuals are treated like robots.

a. Certified in Production and Inventory Management
b. Quality circle
c. Connectionist expert systems
d. Competency-based job descriptions

31. _________ is subcontracting a process, such as product design or manufacturing, to a third-party company. The decision to outsource is often made in the interest of lowering cost or making better use of time and energy costs, redirecting or conserving energy directed at the competencies of a particular business, or to make more efficient use of land, labor, capital, (information) technology and resources. _________ became part of the business lexicon during the 1980s.

a. Unemployment insurance
b. Operant conditioning
c. Opinion leadership
d. Outsourcing

32. _________ is the incidence or process of transferring ownership of a business, enterprise, agency or public service from the public sector (government) to the private sector (business.) In a broader sense, _________ refers to transfer of any government function to the private sector including governmental functions like revenue collection and law enforcement.

a. Performance reports
b. Privatization
c. 1990 Clean Air Act
d. 28-hour day

33. _________ is an advertisement in which a particular product specifically mentions a competitor by name for the express purpose of showing why the competitor is inferior to the product naming it.

This should not be confused with parody advertisements, where a fictional product is being advertised for the purpose of poking fun at the particular advertisement, nor should it be confused with the use of a coined brand name for the purpose of comparing the product without actually naming an actual competitor. ('Wikipedia tastes better and is less filling than the Encyclopedia Galactica.')

In the 1980s, during what has been referred to as the cola wars, soft-drink manufacturer Pepsi ran a series of advertisements where people, caught on hidden camera, in a blind taste test, chose Pepsi over rival Coca-Cola.

a. 33 Strategies of War
b. 1990 Clean Air Act
c. 28-hour day
d. Comparative advertising

34. _________ is an effective method of monitoring a process through the use of control charts. Control charts enable the use of objective criteria for distinguishing background variation from events of significance based on statistical techniques. Much of its power lies in the ability to monitor both process center and its variation about that center.

a. Process capability
b. Quality control
c. Single Minute Exchange of Die
d. Statistical process control

35. _________ is a business management strategy, initially implemented by Motorola, that today enjoys widespread application in many sectors of industry.

_________ seeks to improve the quality of process outputs by identifying and removing the causes of defects (errors) and variation in manufacturing and business processes. It uses a set of quality management methods, including statistical methods, and creates a special infrastructure of people within the organization ('Black Belts' etc.)

a. Six Sigma
b. Production line
c. Takt time
d. Theory of constraints

36. _________ is an organization's process of defining its strategy and making decisions on allocating its resources to pursue this strategy, including its capital and people. Various business analysis techniques can be used in _________, including SWOT analysis (Strengths, Weaknesses, Opportunities, and Threats) and PEST analysis (Political, Economic, Social, and Technological analysis) or STEER analysis involving Socio-cultural, Technological, Economic, Ecological, and Regulatory factors and EPISTEL (Environment, Political, Informatic, Social, Technological, Economic and Legal)

_________ is the formal consideration of an organization's future course. All _________ deals with at least one of three key questions:

1. 'What do we do?'
2. 'For whom do we do it?'
3. 'How do we excel?'

In business _________, the third question is better phrased 'How can we beat or avoid competition?'. (Bradford and Duncan, page 1.)

a. 33 Strategies of War
b. 1990 Clean Air Act
c. 28-hour day
d. Strategic Planning

37. _________ is a reduction in the value of a currency with respect to other monetary units. In common modern usage, it specifically implies an official lowering of the value of a country's currency within a fixed exchange rate system, by which the monetary authority formally sets a new fixed rate with respect to a foreign reference currency. In contrast, depreciation is used for the unofficial decrease in the exchange rate in a floating exchange rate system.

a. 28-hour day
b. 1990 Clean Air Act
c. 33 Strategies of War
d. Devaluation

38. _________ can be regarded as an outcome of mental processes (cognitive process) leading to the selection of a course of action among several alternatives. Every _________ process produces a final choice. The output can be an action or an opinion of choice.

a. 1990 Clean Air Act
b. Decision making
c. 33 Strategies of War
d. 28-hour day

39. A _________ is a set of categories designed to elicit information about a quantitative or a qualitative attribute. In the social sciences, common examples are the Likert scale and 1-10 _________s in which a person selects the number which is considered to reflect the perceived quality of a product.

A _________ is an instrument that requires the rater to assign the rated object that have numerals assigned to them.

a. Spearman-Brown prediction formula
b. Thurstone scale
c. Polytomous Rasch model
d. Rating scale

40. The _________ is an agency of the United States Department of Health and Human Services and is responsible for regulating and supervising the safety of foods, dietary supplements, drugs, vaccines, biological medical products, blood products, medical devices, radiation-emitting devices, veterinary products, and cosmetics. The FDA also enforces section 361 of the Public Health Service Act and the associated regulations, including sanitation requirements on interstate travel as well as specific rules for control of disease on products ranging from pet turtles to semen donations for assisted reproductive medicine techniques.

The FDA is an agency within the United States Department of Health and Human Services responsible for protecting and promoting the nation's public health.

a. Food and Drug Administration
b. 1990 Clean Air Act
c. 28-hour day
d. 33 Strategies of War

41. _________ is the strategic and coherent approach to the management of an organisation's most valued assets - the people working there who individually and collectively contribute to the achievement of the objectives of the business. The terms '_________' and 'human resources' (HR) have largely replaced the term 'personnel management' as a description of the processes involved in managing people in organizations. In simple sense, _________ means employing people, developing their resources, utilizing, maintaining and compensating their services in tune with the job and organizational requirement.

a. Job knowledge
b. Progressive discipline
c. Revolving door syndrome
d. Human resource management

42. _________ has been described as the 'process of social influence in which one person can enlist the aid and support of others in the accomplishment of a common task' . A definition more inclusive of followers comes from Alan Keith of Genentech who said '_________ is ultimately about creating a way for people to contribute to making something extraordinary happen.'

_________ is one of the most salient aspects of the organizational context. However, defining _________ has been challenging.

a. Situational leadership
b. 28-hour day
c. 1990 Clean Air Act
d. Leadership

43. _________ is an organized social movement and market-based approach that aims to help producers in developing countries and promote sustainability. The movement advocates the payment of a higher price to producers as well as social and environmental standards in areas related to the production of a wide variety of goods. It focuses in particular on exports from developing countries to developed countries, most notably handicrafts, coffee, cocoa, sugar, tea, bananas, honey, cotton, wine, fresh fruit, chocolate and flowers.

a. 33 Strategies of War
b. Fair Trade
c. 1990 Clean Air Act
d. 28-hour day

44. _________ is a term used to classify a group leadership theories that inquire the interactions between leaders and followers. A transactional leader focuses more on a series of 'transactions'. This person is interested in looking out for oneself, having exchange benefits with their subordinates and clarify a sense of duty with rewards and punishments to reach goals.

a. 33 Strategies of War
b. Transactional leadership
c. 28-hour day
d. 1990 Clean Air Act

Chapter 1

1. d	2. b	3. d	4. d	5. d	6. a	7. d	8. c	9. d	10. c
11. d	12. b	13. d	14. c	15. a	16. d	17. d	18. a	19. d	20. c
21. d	22. c	23. d	24. c	25. a	26. a	27. d	28. d	29. b	30. d
31. d	32. a	33. c	34. d	35. c	36. d	37. d	38. b	39. d	40. d
41. d									

Chapter 2

1. d	2. c	3. d	4. d	5. d	6. b	7. d	8. d	9. d	10. b
11. d	12. c	13. a	14. b	15. b	16. d	17. c	18. a	19. c	20. d
21. d	22. c	23. b	24. d	25. a	26. d	27. a	28. d	29. d	30. d
31. a	32. b	33. d	34. c	35. a	36. d	37. b	38. d	39. d	

Chapter 3

1. c	2. a	3. d	4. a	5. d	6. a	7. a	8. d	9. d	10. b
11. d	12. d	13. d	14. c	15. a	16. d	17. d	18. b	19. b	20. d
21. d	22. b	23. a	24. d	25. d	26. d	27. d	28. a	29. c	30. a
31. d	32. a	33. d	34. d	35. b	36. d	37. b	38. a	39. d	40. d
41. d	42. d	43. d	44. b	45. d	46. b	47. a			

Chapter 4

1. d	2. d	3. b	4. d	5. c	6. d	7. a	8. a	9. d	10. a
11. d	12. a	13. d	14. d	15. a	16. b	17. c	18. d	19. c	20. a
21. d	22. b	23. b	24. c	25. c	26. b	27. d	28. d	29. d	30. b
31. d	32. a	33. c	34. c	35. b	36. d	37. c	38. d	39. c	40. a
41. b	42. d	43. d	44. b						

Chapter 5

1. d	2. b	3. d	4. d	5. d	6. d	7. c	8. b	9. b	10. d
11. d	12. d	13. d	14. d	15. b	16. d	17. c	18. a	19. a	20. a
21. b	22. b	23. b	24. d						

Chapter 6

1. d	2. a	3. a	4. d	5. c	6. d	7. c	8. d	9. a	10. a
11. b	12. b	13. a	14. d	15. d	16. d	17. a	18. d	19. d	20. d
21. a	22. a	23. d	24. a	25. b	26. d	27. a	28. d	29. d	30. d
31. b	32. d	33. d	34. d	35. d					

Chapter 7

1. d	2. c	3. d	4. d	5. d	6. a	7. d	8. d	9. d	10. d
11. a	12. b	13. a	14. d	15. b	16. c	17. c	18. a	19. d	20. d
21. d	22. d	23. b	24. d	25. c	26. d	27. d	28. c	29. a	30. b
31. d									

Chapter 8

1. a	2. d	3. d	4. a	5. c	6. d	7. a	8. b	9. b	10. c
11. d	12. a	13. c	14. c	15. d	16. a	17. a	18. b	19. a	20. a
21. d	22. a	23. d	24. a	25. a	26. b	27. b	28. b	29. c	30. d
31. d	32. b	33. b	34. b	35. d	36. b	37. d	38. d	39. d	

Chapter 9

1. a	2. d	3. a	4. d	5. c	6. d	7. c	8. b	9. d	10. d
11. d	12. d	13. d	14. d	15. d	16. b	17. c	18. d	19. d	20. b
21. d	22. b	23. b	24. d	25. c	26. a	27. a	28. d	29. a	30. d
31. d	32. a	33. a	34. a	35. d	36. a	37. c	38. a	39. b	40. d
41. d	42. b	43. d	44. a	45. d	46. d	47. c	48. d	49. d	50. d
51. a	52. c	53. d	54. a	55. d	56. a	57. b	58. c		

Chapter 10

1. b	2. d	3. d	4. d	5. d	6. d	7. a	8. d	9. b	10. d
11. a	12. a	13. c	14. d	15. d	16. d	17. d	18. d	19. a	20. a
21. c	22. d								

Chapter 11

1. b	2. b	3. c	4. c	5. c	6. a	7. d	8. a	9. d	10. b
11. d	12. d	13. d	14. b	15. b	16. d	17. c	18. d	19. a	20. d
21. a	22. b	23. d	24. a	25. d	26. d	27. d	28. d	29. d	30. d
31. d	32. d	33. d	34. a	35. d	36. b	37. d	38. d	39. d	

Chapter 12

1. b	2. a	3. a	4. d	5. d	6. c	7. a	8. d	9. d	10. b
11. a	12. a	13. b	14. c	15. d	16. d	17. c	18. d	19. c	20. d
21. d	22. a	23. d	24. d	25. b	26. c	27. d	28. c	29. d	30. b
31. d	32. b	33. a	34. d	35. b	36. c	37. b	38. a	39. d	40. a
41. d	42. d	43. c							

Chapter 13

1. c	2. d	3. c	4. d	5. a	6. d	7. d	8. c	9. d	10. d
11. d	12. c	13. a	14. a	15. c	16. d	17. b	18. d	19. a	20. b
21. b	22. b	23. a	24. c	25. c	26. d	27. d	28. d		

Chapter 14

1. d	2. d	3. d	4. d	5. a	6. a	7. b	8. b	9. d	10. d
11. b	12. a	13. b	14. a	15. c	16. c	17. b	18. d	19. d	20. d
21. b	22. d	23. b	24. d	25. a	26. d	27. b	28. b	29. b	30. d
31. d	32. a	33. b							

Chapter 15

1. b	2. d	3. b	4. d	5. b	6. d	7. a	8. a	9. b	10. c
11. d	12. d	13. c	14. c	15. d	16. b	17. a	18. d	19. a	20. d
21. d	22. d	23. a	24. d						

Chapter 16

1. d	2. a	3. d	4. a	5. d	6. b	7. a	8. a	9. d	10. d
11. b	12. d	13. d	14. b	15. a	16. a	17. d	18. b	19. b	20. d
21. d	22. b	23. a	24. a	25. a	26. a	27. b	28. d	29. c	30. b
31. d	32. b	33. d	34. d	35. a	36. d	37. d	38. b	39. d	40. a
41. d	42. d	43. b	44. b						

www.ingramcontent.com/pod-product-compliance
Lightning Source LLC
Chambersburg PA
CBHW082044230426
43670CB00016B/2767
* 9 7 8 1 4 2 8 8 7 0 4 1 3 *